ECHOES FROM FRI
CRITICALLY ENGAGE

Available from Bloomsbury:

On Critical Pedagogy, by Henry A. Giroux
Critical Pedagogy and Social Justice, by John Smyth

Forthcoming:

Rethinking Citizenship, by Kevin D. Vinson and E. Wayne Ross
Pedagogy of Beauty, by Antonia Darder
Narrative, Learning, and Critical Pedagogy, by Ivor Goodson and Scherto Gill

ECHOES FROM FREIRE FOR A CRITICALLY ENGAGED PEDAGOGY

PETER MAYO

BLOOMSBURY
NEW YORK • LONDON • NEW DELHI • SYDNEY

Bloomsbury Academic
An imprint of Bloomsbury Publishing Plc

175 Fifth Avenue
New York
NY 10010
USA

50 Bedford Square
London
WC1B 3DP
UK

www.bloomsbury.com

First published 2013

Library of Congress Cataloging-in-Publication Data
A catalog record for this book is available from the Library of Congress.

ISBN: HB: 978-1-4411-1817-2
PB: 978-1-4411-1085-5
PDF: 978-1-4411-4301-3
ePub: 978-1-4411-3730-2

Typeset by Newgen Imaging Systems Pvt Ltd, Chennai, India
Printed and bound in the United States of America

Contents

Acknowledgements

I would like to thank my wife Josephine Mayo and daughters, Annemarie Mayo and Cecilia Mayo, for their love and support as I worked through the various articles that constitute the basis for this book.

I would like to thank a number of people whose ideas inspired me to write this book: Paula Allman (late), Federico Batini, Carmel Borg, Mario Cardona, Mary Darmanin, Antonia Darder, Antonia De Vita, Leona M. English, Henry A. Giroux, Budd L. Hall, Dip Kapoor, Margaret Ledwith, Peter McLaren, André Elias Mazawi, Anna Maria Piussi, students in my MA Adult Education classes at University of Malta (2008, 2010 cohorts), students in the MA Adult Education graduate class at University of Seville in 2007, students in my graduate class at Bogazici University in July 2009, students in my PGCE classes on Freire from 2009 till 2011, students in my comparative adult education class at UBC in July 2010, Alessio Surian, Bruno Schettini (late), Daniel Schugurensky, Shirley Steinberg, Carlos Alberto Torres and Kenneth Wain.

I also need to acknowledge prior publication of chapters either in their current or revised form in a number of other outlets, ranging from journals to conference proceedings.

Chapter 1 is based on an article in the Classic Texts Commentary Series, published as Mayo, P. (2010), 'Signposts for a Politically Engaged Pedagogy', *Community Development Journal*, Vol. 45, No. 3, pp. 380–4.

Chapter 2 is based on a short article, published as Mayo, P. (2008), 'Tenth Anniversary of Paulo Freire's Death. On Whose Side Are We When We Teach/Act?', *Adult Education and Development*, No. 69, pp. 105–11.

Chapter 3 is based on an entry in Portuguese, published as Mayo, P. (2010), 'Intellectuais', in D. Streck, E. Redin and J. J. Zitkoski (Eds), *Dicionário Paulo Freire,* Belo Horizonte: Autêntica Editora.

Chapter 4 is a revised version of a chapter which first appeared as Mayo, P. (2008), 'Reading and Transforming the World Together. A Freirean Perspective on Education and Social Movements', in *Revista de stiinte ale educatiei*, anul 10, 1(17), pp. 66–8. It provided the basis for a much larger and much more amplified version, which appeared as a co-authored chapter (ch. 10) 'Adult Education and Social Movements', in L. English and P. Mayo (2012), *Learning with Adults. A Critical Pedagogical Introduction*, Rotterdam and Taipei: Sense Publishers; it also appeared as an article English, L. and Mayo, P. (2012), 'Adult Education and Social Movements: Perspectives from Freire and Beyond', *Educazione Democratica*, Nu. 3, pp. 170–208, also available online: www.educazionedemocratica.it/.

Chapter 5 was previously published as Mayo, P. (2010), 'The Competence Discourse in Education and the Struggle for Social Agency and Critical Citizenship', *International Journal of Educational Policies*, Vol. 3, No. 2, pp. 5–16.

Chapter 6 was originally published in Portuguese as Mayo, P. (2005), 'Educação Critica e Desenvolvimento de uma Cidadania Multi- Étnica. Uma perspective a partir do Sul da Europa', *Revista Lusófona de Educação*, No. 6, pp. 47–54.

Chapter 7 was originally published as Mayo, P. (2010), 'Popular Education and Transformative Research', in Emilio Lucio-Villegas (Ed.), *Transforming/Researching Communities*, Xátiva: Dialogos-Red, ESREA.

Chapter 8 is a revised version of Mayo, P. (2010), 'Adult Learning, Instruction and Programme Planning – A Freirean Perspective', in Penelope Peterson, Eva Baker and Barry McGaw (Eds.), *International Encyclopedia of Education*, Volume 1, pp. 31–5. Oxford: Elsevier.

Chapter 9 is a revised and whittled down version of Mayo, P. (2007), 'Critical Approaches to Education in the Work of Lorenzo Milani and Paulo Freire', *Studies in Philosophy and Education*, Vol. 26, No. 6, pp. 525–44.

Chapter 10 is a slightly revised version of the paper Mayo, P. (2001), 'Julius Nyerere (1922–1999) and Education – A Tribute', *International Journal of Educational Development*, Vol. 21, No. 3, pp. 193–202.

Chapter 11 is a revised and much amplified version of Mayo, P. (2010), 'Obituary Dr Paula Allman', *Policy Futures in Education*, Vol. 9, No. 5, pp. 661–2.

Chapter 13 originally appeared as Mayo, P. (2010), 'Striving Against the Eclipse of Democracy Henry A. Giroux's Critical Pedagogy for Social Justice', *Italian Journal of Sociology of Education*, No. 3, pp. 254–82.

FREIREAN CONCEPTS

CHAPTER 1

Introduction

Pedagogy of the Oppressed: Anniversary Tribute for an Anniversary Series

In 1980, I had been concluding my studies to become a teacher. I recall having participated, at the time, in a course-unit in which groups of students gave presentations on different authors whose views influenced educational thinking. My choice fell on Jean Jacques Rousseau. I do recall, however, having listened to one presentation which focused on excerpts from a very intriguing text written by a Brazilian whose name remained etched in my memory. Whatever was being presented somehow captured my imagination. After graduation, I was posted at a school situated in a particular district of my home city Valletta and I found the going tough. Looking back I wonder whether my teaching would have been better served had the title *Pedagogy of the Oppressed* not remained simply an intriguing one and had the book not been earmarked as a 'must read' for the future, since my reading had then and in subsequent years been taken up by literary classics.

When I eventually got down to reading *Pedagogy of the Oppressed* (henceforth *Pedagogy*), I had already taught in the Maltese educational system for a number of years. In hindsight, I would say that many of the pupils I taught, certainly those in my first school in Valletta, represented classic cases of boys and girls immersed in the 'culture of silence'. I had hitherto demonstrated little understanding of the class, gender and racial politics of our educational system, the kind of 'cultural invasion' teachers like myself perpetrated and the often superficial kind of interactive pedagogy in which I engaged, often taking the form of simply eliciting information and views – a far cry from Freire's notion of authentic dialogue. My emphasis was more on problem solving than problem posing. And to make matters worse, the notion of exploring and 'learning' the community in which one teaches was completely alien to me. Furthermore, learning was by and large viewed as an individual and not a collective activity.

The occasion for reading *Pedagogy* was the start of my graduate studies in Alberta, Canada, and the book certainly proved a revelation to me. It seemed to contain many of the insights and elements necessary for me to understand the context in which my previous teaching in Malta had taken place. These included subalternity, colonial legacies, relative poverty, class issues (including language issues) and issues concerning racism (there were African Maltese students in our school at a time when Maltese society was nowhere near the multi-ethnic society it has become in recent years).

Freire's work, together with those of Marx, Gramsci, Nyerere and a number of exponents of critical pedagogy and the 'new sociology of education', which I started studying at the time, helped bring about a 'perspective transformation' in me. I would dare say that Freire's was a very significant influence on my view of the world from then onwards. While many other writers appealed to me mostly at a cerebral level, he was among a selection of writers who 'spoke to me' also at an emotional level.

The book helped me develop sensitivity to the politics of knowledge and to confront a very disturbing question: on whose side am I when I teach/act? And the complexities of the relationship between oppressor and oppressed, as indicated by Freire in his discussion of the Oppressor Consciousness, the 'oppressor within', make me tread warily when answering this question (see Fischman, 2009). I began to realize that this involves not a neat binary opposition between oppressors and oppressed but a dialectical relationship. Freire's challenge to me, through this book, was to make me try to think dialectically, to avoid linear, simplistic conceptions of the relationship between people (Allman, 1999). He also taught me to appreciate the virtues of and ethical issues involved in dialogical education and to realize that this approach to learning, once again based on a dialectical engagement with the material world, implies not a *laissez-faire* pedagogy but one that is directive (his later distinction between authority and authoritarianism in teaching would enable me to understand this better). I also learnt from Freire and his book the central place that must be devoted to the Aristotelian notion of *praxis*, of education involving reflection upon action for transformative action – enabling ourselves and our co-learners to take critical distance from what we know to perceive it in a more critical light. This is a far cry from the conventionally acceptable but ultimately culturally alienating way in which I taught in the postcolonial Maltese context. Here the language of instruction and especially assessment for certain subjects was English, not the national-popular Maltese language, a situation that obtains in a number of postcolonial states (see Freire's experience in Guinea Bissau). This often militates against praxis, rendering it culturally alienating to pupils not exposed to this language as part of their *habitus*.

Although social class considerations, such as these, retain their importance within a critical approach to education, there are other considerations of social difference to be borne in mind. In this regard, one cannot but appreciate Freire's engagement with feminist and anti-racist issues in his reaction to criticisms of *Pedagogy*. The book should therefore be treated as a classic which needs to be read alongside these criticisms and Freire's responses to them. Indeed it is the sort of classic that committed feminist and anti-racist writers such as bell hooks found instructive despite its 'phallocentric' view of liberation, hence hooks' incorporation of insights from this text and *Education for Critical Consciousness* in her well-known works *Talking Back* and *Teaching to Transgress*.

For someone like me who was brought up and still lives in a country with a long history of what Said (1993, p. 8) calls *direct* colonialism, applied to situations characterized by the presence of an occupying force, reading *Pedagogy*, where the discussion on oppression and liberation is carried out against a rich backdrop of insights from the history of Brazilian and Latin American colonization (predicated on racist human expropriation and extermination), meant something else. It meant much to read Freire extensively and intensively after having been brought up reading texts primarily by mainstream European (mainly British) and American authors. Reading Freire, a 'southern' author, and other 'majority world' writers, taught my 'colonized mind' a lot about the social dimensions of knowledge and the need for its de-colonization through reading, thinking and acting beyond the exclusively eurocentric framework. It is also interesting to see how the obvious anthropocentric nature of *Pedagogy*, which once drew forth a strong adverse reaction from some of my animal loving students at University, contrasts with Freire's much later work (dealing with the theme of environmental degradation in the 'popular public' community schools he administered as Education Secretary in São Paulo) and that of his followers who brought an ecological dimension to his ideas (Gadotti, 2005; Gutierrez and Cruz Prado, 2000; Kahn, 2006).

Of course the relevance of Freire's work to my context, a Catholic Church dominated context, extends beyond *Pedagogy* to incorporate later works such as those focusing on the Prophetic, as opposed to the traditional/Constantinian/modernizing, church (see Cornell West on this).

Pedagogy of the Oppressed remains a classic in the fields of education, political mobilization and community development. One must however complement the reading of this book with the reading of other and later works by Freire and exponents of Freire-influenced critical pedagogy to develop a more holistic view of the kind of politically engaged pedagogy he helped inspire.

I am therefore honored to have been invited by the editors of this series to contribute a book to a series commemorating the fortieth anniversary of the publication of this classic text. I sought to answer this call by revisiting a number of pieces I have written over the years through which echoes from Freire strongly reverberate. In Chapter 2, I will outline some of the basic concepts in Freire's philosophy and pedagogical approach to which references will be made in the various chapters that follow. I will then discuss briefly Freire's ideas concerning the role of critical intellectuals and public life, drawing on his own writings that are pertinent to the topic. This will be followed by a section in which key issues regarding education and social activism will be viewed from a Freirean perspective. The selection includes issues relating to the current hegemonic competence discourse in education, learning in social movements and the development of a critical multi-ethnic cultural democracy. I will then move on to provide a Freirean perspective on research, specifically transformative research, and programme planning, with a focus on adult education. The final two sections focus on personages with whose ideas and formulations Freire's concepts can be compared. In an earlier work, I compared Freire's ideas with those of Antonio Gramsci. This time I focus on a person whom Freire knew and with whom he wanted to collaborate, Tanzania's first president, Julius Kambarage Nyerere. This chapter is intended to provide an African perspective on some of the issues, such as colonialism and educational legacies and indigenous knowledge, which have been addressed by Freire. I also provide a comparative piece focusing on Freire and the Italian critical educator Lorenzo Milani, given that there are strong affinities between the works of both and that they are often mentioned in the same breath in Milani's Italy. The final section remains true to the book's title by highlighting the ideas of three persons who, although being major educators and educationists in their own right, draw inspiration from Freire: Antonia Darder, Henry Giroux and the late Paula Allman.

CHAPTER 2

Freire's Ideas More Generally: On Whose Side Are We When We Teach and Act?

Paulo Reglus Neves Freire (1921–97) has achieved iconic status among educators and a whole range of cultural workers striving for greater social justice and who imagine a world not as it is now but as it should and can be.

Born in Recife, in the state of Pernambuco in the impoverished Nord-Este of Brazil, Paulo Freire dedicated the best part of his life to combating social injustices in various parts of the world and educating/learning *with* the oppressed he came across in the various contexts in which he was active. He suffered imprisonment and exile for his efforts in planning what was perceived as being a 'subversive' approach to literacy in Brazil in the early 1960s. He moved briefly to Bolivia and then to Chile where he was engaged in an educational programme connected with the agrarian reform, and the United States where he had his major work *Pedagogia do Oprimido* (Pedagogy of the Oppressed) published in English translation. He eventually went to Geneva where he worked for the World Council of Churches. He was frequently called upon by revolutionary governments, such as those in Guinea Bissau, to assist them in developing and evaluating educational projects. He also used his 16-year period of exile to work with a variety of groups in different parts of Europe and also engaged, following the *abertura* and his return to Brazil from exile, in the complex area of municipal educational administration in São Paulo. He was also a most prolific writer; many of his works were translated into English and other languages. Books by him continued to be published throughout the last 10 years, including the most recent English translation of *Pedagogia da Indignação* (Pedagogy of Indignation) and *Pedagogia da Tolerancia*. Freire's better-known work, *Pedagogy of the Oppressed*, is regarded by many to be exemplary in the way it comprises reflections on the various contexts with which he was engaged. In this work Freire constantly provides theoretical formulations and insights deriving from a variety of sources. The key aspect of Freire's work is the emphasis on the political nature of education: education *is* politics. For Freire refutes the view that education can be neutral. He argues that education can either 'domesticate' or 'liberate'. And a liberating education is one that fosters the disposition among learners to engage in a dialectical relationship with knowledge and society.

A unidirectional, 'top-to-bottom' process of teacher–student transmission, which is often symptomatic of a wider prescriptive process of communication, constitutes a domesticating education ('banking education'). Freire advocates an authentically dialogical approach to knowledge. His is a complex notion of dialogue. Although not being on an equal footing, teacher and learner learn from each other as they co-investigate dialectically the object of knowledge. The concept that lies at the heart of this process is praxis, a key term in Freire's work, which dates back to the time of the Ancient Greeks, including the work of Aristotle. It is central to Paulo Freire's educational philosophy. For this reason it will be referred to time and time again in this book. This entails a process whereby learners and educators obtain a critical distance from the world they know to perceive it in a different and critical light. They are encouraged to 'extraordinarily re-experience the ordinary', as critical educator Ira Shor once put it. The community, in which the learning setting is situated, is researched beforehand by a team of educators and project participants (including learners). The research includes informal meetings with members of the community, close observation of their speech patterns, obtaining knowledge of the community members' concerns, and so on. The insights, information and knowledge derived from this research are codified into learning material. This material is intended to enable learners from the same community to obtain critical distance from it to be able to unveil collectively and with the help of the educator, who also learns from these insights and dialogical interactions with the group, the underlying contradictions of the society in question.

Freire places the emphasis on dialogue and on the pedagogy of the question. Knowledge is problematized. Things are called into question in what is a problem posing rather than a problem solving approach. The object of knowledge is an object of co-investigation. Knowledge is therefore not something possessed by the educator which he or she transfers to the learner but is something both educator and learner co-investigate, explore together. Knowledge is therefore conceived of as dynamic rather than static. Learning is regarded as a political process and is directive. The roles of educator and learner are almost interchangeable, as all learn from each other, but this is not to say that the learner and educator are on an equal footing. The latter must have a certain amount of authority (bestowed on the educator by the learner because of the former's competence in the field of learning and as a pedagogue) which should not be allowed to degenerate into authoritarianism lest the spirit of genuine dialogue would be destroyed. Only through dialogue does the group learn collectively to unveil the contradictions that underlie the reality being focused upon. Adult educators are encouraged to show tact when promoting dialogical relations and there are moments when they alternate dialogue with a certain degree of instruction, especially on consideration that people exposed for years to banking education do not engage in dialogue easily. The starting point of co-investigation is the learner's existential reality which is however not the be all and end all of the learning process, lest one would be guilty of populism or *basismo*. Educators must have enough humility to relearn, through their dialogic interactions with the learners, that which they think they already know.

Freire conceived of the educators and learners as 'integral human beings' (Darder, 2002, p. 94) in an educational process based on love (ibid.). Love is a key element in the humanizing relationship between teacher and taught (teacher–student and student–teacher, in Freire's terms). It also lies at the heart of the educator's efforts in teaching and working for the dismantling of dehumanizing structures. Freire is reported to have said just before his death:

> I could never think of education without love and that is why I think I am an educator, first of all because I feel love . . . (In McLaren, 2002)

And the entire pedagogical process practiced and articulated by Freire is based on his trust in human beings and in their ability to create 'a world in which it will be easier to love' (see Allman et al., 1998, p. 9; Freire, 1970a, 1993, p. 40). Freire's concept of love has strong Christian overtones and revolutionary ones. In his early writings Freire even mentioned revolutionary love which he attributed to Che Guevara who, 'did not hesitate to recognize the capacity of love as an indispensable condition for authentic revolutionaries' (Freire, 1970b, p. 45). Freire's impact has been strongly felt among many educators including those operating within progressive, social justice–oriented social movements. The reasons for this are many. The movements are often attracted to Freire's philosophy and pedagogical approach because of the emphases on value commitment ('on whose side are we?'), on praxis, on the collective dimension of learning and liberation, on people capable of being tactically inside and strategically outside the system, on refuting cynicism with the belief that another world is possible (a healthy utopia), on the ongoing quest for greater coherence and on the need for persons to develop and constantly adopt a critical attitude. I shall discuss this in greater detail in a chapter dedicated to social movements. Freire's influence is felt most strongly among the Movimento dos Trabalhadores Rurais Sem Terra (MST) – the landless peasants movement – in his native Brazil. Reference to these concepts will be constantly made throughout the ensuing chapters which will also highlight other concepts from Freire that are most pertinent to the matter at issue. For a fuller exposition of Freire's ideas, I would refer the reader to my earlier book on Freire (Mayo, 2004, 2010). One issue which deserves a short but specific treatment is that concerning Freire's conception of intellectuals since a conscientized educator in Freire's sense as well as a conscientized participant in the learning setting engages in intellectual work. I see Freire's conception being very similar to Gramsci's as I argued in a previous publication (Mayo, 1999). I discuss the issue of intellectuals, from a Freirean perspective, in Chapter 3.

CHAPTER 3

Freire on Intellectuals

Educators and cultural workers influenced by Freire and who work to transform situations and spaces into more democratic ones are often referred to as intellectuals. The literature on critical pedagogy is replete with references to transformative intellectuals (Giroux, 1988), public intellectuals and organic intellectuals (Gramsci, 1971). In this chapter I will attempt to develop, albeit briefly, a Freirean view of 'intellectuals', which I regard as important given that, later on in this volume, I shall be looking closely at the work of people who, in my view, function as intellectuals, some even as public intellectuals, in the sense developed by Freire. The chapter provided the basis for an entry precisely on this topic in the Brazilian version of the Freire dictionary (Streck et al., 2008, p. 227). Its inclusion in the dictionary underlines its importance in Freire's thinking.

Ideas and ruminations on revolutionary intellectual activity abound throughout Freire's entire oeuvre. We have seen how one central concept that emerges from Freire's writing is that revolutionary intellectual activity is characterized by *praxis*, that is reflection on one's world of action for transformation. There will be recurring reference to this concept throughout the rest of the volume given its centrality in Freire's pedagogical politics. This approximates Marx's notion, in the *Theses on Feuerbach*, that the main purpose is not simply to interpret the world but to transform it. Transformation is a key element in Freire's conception of intellectuals which, although it takes into account the function of traditional intellectuals such as those of international acclaim as well as university professors (see his exchanges with professors from UNAM in Escobar et al., 1994), is more on the lines of Gramsci's analysis of the role of intellectuals in society. In short the intellectual is analysed in terms of the role he or she performs in either supporting/cementing the existing hegemonic arrangements or challenging them. In the latter case, the intellectual helps problematize issues, through a problem posing approach to dialogue, that fosters the critical consciousness necessary to help generate social change. The change which Freire advocates is one predicated on social justice. In this respect, Freire's intellectual is very much a transformative intellectual, to adopt the term used by his friend and collaborator Henry A. Giroux (1988), as indicated in the introductory chapter.

The closest reinvention of Gramsci's analysis of the role of intellectuals in revolutionary practice is probably available in the *Letters to Guinea Bissau* (Freire, 1978) and most notably in Letter 11. There, as in other writings, he tackles the issue of the colonial legacy in education which is very elitist and restricts the attainment of qualifications to a small cadre of people who serve as urban intellectuals having close links with and supporting the colonial powers. The influence of Amilcar Cabral, Antonio Gramsci and Karl Marx can be detected in this discussion on intellectuals within the context of an impoverished newly liberated country seeking to rid itself of its colonial shackles. This is the classic 'Third World' situation that Freire confronts in the majority of his writings, especially his better-known ones. He adopts Cabral's notion of the elitist intellectual, in such a situation, having to commit *class suicide* to be born again as a revolutionary worker who identifies with the aspirations of the people. This immediately recalls Gramsci's notion of the revolutionary party and movement assimilating traditional intellectuals to contribute towards the generation of the much aspired 'intellectual and moral reform'. Like Gramsci, however, Freire mentions that it is also necessary to generate from within the ranks of the subaltern a new type of intellectual, whose thinking and activity help generate a new *weltanschauung*. Here Freire's conceptualization recalls Marx's notion of a polytechnical education, espoused in the Geneva Resolution of 1866. Freire advocates that the new type of intellectual should be forged in the unity between practice and theory, manual and intellectual work (shades of Mao) (Freire, 1978, p. 104). Freire does so without discarding the importance of re-educating elitist intellectuals which remains a very important task in the immediate and later postcolonial setting in which the challenge posed is that of 'decolonizing the mind' (elsewhere, Freire quotes the Cape Verde President Aristides Perreira on this; Freire, 1985). Freire however warns that the 'death' of such traditional elitist intellectuals is not easily accepted by those who nevertheless commit themselves to a revolutionary position. Echoing Bourdieu and his notion of *habitus*, he seems to be suggesting that such intellectuals, though ethically committed to the subaltern, find it difficult to 'jump out of their skin' and be with and like them. He points out that the intellectual education of the middle class reinforces the class position of its recipients and, as Gramsci had explained with regard to the role of southern intellectuals in Italy, also with respect to the role language plays in this process (see Ives, 2004), makes them 'absolutize' their activity and conceive of it as being superior to that of those who did not benefit from the same opportunity. For Freire, the challenge in a revolutionary setting, characterized by attempts at what he elsewhere calls the transformation of power, is to not create elitist intellectuals who commit class suicide but prevent their formation in the first place (Freire, 1978, p. 104). The point of departure for intellectuals working *with*, and not on behalf of, the people is the latter's *concrete existential situation*. This entails a search for the thematic complexes that arise from this existential situation. The intellectual activity however entails moving beyond this situation, otherwise this would be a form of populism which maintains people where they are. The learners and educators (in the formal sense since they are all co-learners) need to move forward in their thinking, awareness and overall learning.

The intellectuals analysed by Gramsci, with respect to their function in Italian society and the evolution of its politics, are various, ranging from grand intellectuals who help fashion the cultural climate of the period (Croce, Fortunato) or who through their artistic productions make their mark on the Italian cultural scene (Pirandello) to subaltern intellectuals operating in restricted spheres of influence (priests, lawyers, managers, teachers). Educators play an important role here together with other cultural workers. Freire's writings on the role of the educator in a liberating education are quite pertinent in this respect. The critical educator, in Freire's sense, is a critical intellectual who, because of her/his preparation and competence, has *authority*, is accepted by the participants in the educational setting, but is humble and democratic enough not to allow this authority to degenerate into *authoritarianism*. The critical educator takes a position and *directs* the process of learning, arousing *epistemological curiosity*, but must be open to re-learning from the students who provide different perspectives, often deriving from their respective social location, that have a bearing on the object of co-investigation. In this respect, the intellectual-educator directs a process of intellectual activity, characterized by reflection upon action (praxis), the obtaining of critical distance from the world one knows, in which the intellectual task is shared by one and all – all perform the function of intellectuals, as well as of teachers and learners, though not to the same extent. They learn and teach together and one another in a process that underlines the *collective* dimension of learning and intellectual activity.

FREIREAN INTERPRETATIONS

CHAPTER 4

Reading and Transforming the World Together: A Freirean Perspective on Education and Social Movements

In many places people seem to be falling into disenchantment with political parties especially at the national level, as parties in power fail to deliver on their promises and make too many compromises with transnational corporations and the organizations that regulate trade. The great hope generated by such governments as the Lula Federal Government in Brazil, for instance, often turns into disappointment (see Baeirle in Borg and Mayo, 2007) probably resulting in cynicism; too much is probably expected of these governments before and immediately after they are elected. The same probably applied to Obama's election as president and the chapter on Giroux, at the end, reflects a certain disenchantment with some of the policies he has endorsed, not least the continuation of the 'no child left behind' education programme.

Exposure of corruptive practices in various countries, as with *tangentopoli* in Italy in the early 1990s, continues to portray parties in a bad light. Then there is the sight of parties that were traditionally socialist turning to the Centre or possibly the Right with neoliberalism proving hegemonic since it is embraced by both sides of the political spectrum (Mayo, 1999). Michael Hardt and Antonio Negri (2003) argue that, despite their presence at the World Social Forum at Porto Alegre in 2002, social democratic forces from various countries constitute a problem in terms of linking up with them in an anti-[hegemonic] globalization 'movement of movements' in that their conservative elements have 'thus become inescapably identified with the deepest interests of capitalist power, where exploitation and repression constitute the fundamental political line' (p. xviii). Over the last year and more we have seen people gathering in the squares and streets of Tunisia and Egypt, risking life and limb in the process, clamouring for political change, though the jury is still out on whether they constitute a movement. The situation in Libya is even worse resulting in a civil war and human carnage. Same protests, resulting in deaths, occur in places such as Syria and, of course, we have been witnessing massive protests throughout Europe and North America with regard to a variety of issues such as the debtocracy, malpractices in financial governance and the fact that 1 per cent owns much of the world's wealth. There has been talk of the global movement of the 99 per cent and of indignant masses, especially in the latter case, in Spain and Greece. It remains to be seen what trajectory these actions and protests will take.

The disenchantment with Leftist, especially social democratic, parties has led to faith in social movements as organizations which apply pressure, combat co-optation (though not always) and provide the freedom and non-hierarchical mode of operation not found in political parties. One wonders whether they have been perceived to constitute an alternative to the 'defeated Left' as a result of the collapse of the Berlin Wall. There is a tendency, in my view, to romanticize social movements with their virtues often being 'talked up' rather than providing a fit to reality. Leona English and I provide a discussion on some of the complexities involved elsewhere (English and Mayo, 2012).

Social movements are often presented as being less hierarchical than traditional political organizations such as political parties, though trade unions, often regarded as forming part of a larger 'old' social movement, the Labour Movement, are likewise hierarchical. Traditionally, social movements by and large focus on specific issues and allow room for popular participation. They also comprise a variety of organizations and individuals.

Because of the above attributes and their emphasis on popular participation, dialogue, conscientization and *denúncia-anúncio*, some social movements focusing on social justice issues can easily draw inspiration from Paulo Freire, among other figures. These other figures are legion. I would single out Gramsci from among them.

One cannot talk about social movements without mentioning the Gramscian concept of *Hegemony*, which was used by others before and during Gramsci's time. Gramsci uses hegemony frequently, even though he never provides a systematic exposition of the concept. In my view, one of the best definitions of Hegemony, used in the Gramscian sense, is provided by the Canadian sociologist David W. Livingstone. He defines Hegemony as: 'a social condition in which all aspects of social reality are dominated by or supportive of a single class' or group (Livingstone, 1976, p. 235).

In an interview with Roger Dale and Susan Robertson (Dale and Robertson, 2006, p. 148), Boaventura de Sousa Santos talks of two kinds of globalization. He refers to 'hegemonic globalisation', used in a manner that renders this term akin to that of 'globalisation from above' (Marshall, 1997), and 'counter-hegemonic globalisation' (or 'globalization from below' to use the more popular phrase). The first type of globalization is that which the more progressive, social justice–oriented social movements confront. The second provides the context for international networking among these movements. I would argue that the two are to be seen not as binary opposites but as existing in a dialectical relationship. The former seeks to enhance its dynamism by drawing on the latter (appropriating an oppositional discourse as part of gradual renewal – e.g. today's oppositional or revolutionary figure becomes tomorrow's commercial icon) while, as Foucault wrote, there can be no power without resistance but this resistance is never external to the power structure itself. Resistance groups of different ideological orientation use the instruments of globalization to get their message across, mobilize, recruit and strike.

Hegemonic globalization is characterized by the following features, among others: Mobility of capital and labour not occurring on a level playing field; the presence of multiple regional markets and the occurrence of fast-paced economic and financial exchange; increasing privatization and therefore the ideology of marketplace; the dismantling of the welfare state and re-mantling of the state to create the infrastructure for investment and mobility, develop the necessary human resources and exert a policing role. The last mentioned task entails controlling what goes on within and on the country's borders through the presence of a 'carceral state' (Giroux, 2004) – surveillance techniques, prisons, immigrant detention centres.

The underlying ideology of this type of globalization – hegemonic globalization – is neoliberalism, which partly owes its origins to such economists as Milton Friedman and which had a sort of 'trial run' in the Pinochet-dictatorship governed Chile in the 1970s. It made its way there via the Chicago Boys, students of Friedman who worked in the Ministry of Economic Development. Boaventura de Sousa Santos defines neoliberalism as '. . . the political form of globalization resulting from a US type of capitalism, a type that bases competitiveness on technological innovation coupled with low levels of social protection' (in Dale and Robertson, 2004, p. 151). Neoliberal globalization is referred to by progressives as the 'empire', in Hardt and Negri's (2000) terms, an empire 'built and maintained' by the IMF, The World Bank, the WTO, 'corporations, banks and the Group of Eight' and sustained by the 'Washington Consensus' (Ponniah and Fisher, 2003, pp. 6–7).

Counter-hegemonic globalization comprises the work of progressive social movements and NGOs, including the efforts of the anti-globalization movements in such places as Seattle,

Davos, Genoa and Chiapas. It particularly includes the work of the major counterweight to the institutions of hegemonic globalization (the World Economic Forum, the WTO and the Breton Woods institutions, namely the IMF and the World Bank). This major counterweight is provided by the World Social Forum (Fisher and Ponniah, 2003) and its regional offshoots such as the Mediterranean Social Forum. Porto Alegre seems to be, nowadays, the spiritual home of those social movements who have met there to form part of the 'movement of movements' (Hardt and Negri, 2003; OSAL and CLACSO, 2003) or the 'network of networks'. In this city, well known for its participatory budget that entails citizenship learning, a 'new internationalism' was said to be born (Hardt and Negri, 2003, p. xvii). This coming together of social movements, including the trade union movement, represents the 'beginning of the democracy of the multitude', once again in Hardt and Negri's terms (2003, p. xix).

Among the many movements worldwide inspired by the World Social Forum, we would find the MST, which has a following in places outside Brazil (e.g. Italy, see Stédile and Fernandes, 2001), the *Frente Zapatista* in Chiapas, the Living Democracy movement in India (see Shiva, 2003, pp. 120–4), the Adivasi movement in India together with a host of other subaltern social movements in southern contexts (see Kapoor, 2009), the feminist, LGBTQ (Lesbian, Gay, Bisexual, Transgendered, Queer), environmental and 'justice in trade' movements and those movements interacting internationally to put pressure on governments to comply with Millennium Development Goals (MDGs) and to make good on their one time promise, in the early 1970s, to reserve 0.7 per cent of their GDP for international aid. The list is not exhaustive.

International networking, as a form of 'globalization from below', often entails using technology for counter-hegemonic ends and might also involve learning informations and communication technology (ICT), public speaking and project promotion skills. However the movements involved in such action, as part of an anti-neoliberal globalization process, are not always progressive and are not always the sort that would be identified with Porto Alegre and the World Social Forum. Globalization of the hegemonic kind marginalizes all sorts of people and discourses and the persons involved resort to different kinds of politics and actions. Some challenge NAFTA (North American Free Trade Agreement) by making radically progressive use of the internet for social justice ends, with all the educational and consciousness raising ramifications this has. They wage an 'internet war' as in the case of the Frente Zapatista in Chiapas. Others, of a much different political orientation, resort to religious fundamentalism or militant forms of religious beliefs such as Militant Islam. *Al Qaeda* is one such movement which promotes and uses learning for terrorist activities, including learning and consciousness raising through the internet, which also serves its purpose for the movement to recruit would-be terrorists. Others react to the loss of security, through the opening and liberalization of borders and the massive demographic shifts that globalization entails, by retrenching into an ultra-nationalist and fascist politics resulting in racist and xenophobic movements against immigration. Vandana Shiva (2003) is particularly instructive in this regard: 'Democracy emptied of economic freedom and ecological freedom becomes a potent breeding-ground for fundamentalism and terrorism. Over the past two decades, I have witnessed conflicts over development and over natural resources mutate into communal conflicts, culminating in extremism and terrorism' (p. 122).

Paulo Freire appeals to the radical social justice side of the social movements' phenomenon. His focus is on education for social justice. Furthermore he advocates and develops an entire philosophy around praxis. Reflection upon action is the sort of process of *conscientização* that would enable social movements to allow their adherents to 'come into consciousness' (Freire, 1993,

p. 110) with regard to certain issues or combination of issues. It serves as the means for one to engage consciously and reflectively on social action and to work effectively for change within his/her specific site of action. The person might at times operate 'in and against the system' (London and Edinburgh Weekend Return Group, 1979, 1980) in which he/she is employed as an educator; being 'tactically inside and strategically outside' the system. Praxis involves a critical reading of the world one inhabits. This is the prerequisite for the sort of 'action for change' that generates greater social justice. Adult Educators operating within social movements can potentially enable people to read not only the word but also the world (Freire and Macedo, 1987).

Freire also stresses the collective dimension of knowledge, the kind of knowledge sharing resulting from and contributing to the type of social solidarity and bonding that the more progressive social movements strive to promote. The less hierarchical nature of the more progressive social movements lends itself to the kind of authentic dialogue that Freire sought. While expertise is often availed of within movements, the *authority* (Freire, in Freire and Macedo, 1995, p. 378) that is bestowed on ethically committed experts is not allowed to degenerate into *authoritarianism* (see, for instance, Freire, in Shor and Freire, 1987, p. 91; Freire, in Horton and Freire, 1990, p. 181; Freire, 1994, p. 79).

Freire gave great prominence to progressive social movements in his work. He constantly exhorted educators to work not in isolation but in the context of social movements or an alliance of movements. Drawing on his own experience as education secretary in São Paulo, where he sought to bring state and movements closer, without one co-opting the other, he explored the potential relationship between party and movements. In a dialogue with academics from UNAM (National Autonomous University of Mexico), he is on record as having said that the Workers' Party (PT), of which he was a founding member, must learn from social movements without trying to take them over. If the Party does so, it will grow:

> Today, if the Workers' Party approaches the popular movements from which it was born, without trying to take them over, the party will grow; if it turns away from the popular movements, in my opinion, the party will wear down. Besides, those movements need to make their struggle politically viable. (Freire, in Escobar et al., 1994, p. 40)

This insight is quite interesting given the criticism often levelled at social movement theorists, namely that they tend to ignore the role of the party, probably, as stated earlier, because of their disenchantment with parties. For instance, authors such as John Holst (2001, p. 112) have argued that social movements activists writing on the relevance of Antonio Gramsci's ideas for adult education tend to ignore the central role which Gramsci attributed to the party (the Modern Prince) in the process of social transformation. The kind of relationship which Freire calls for with regard to party and movements, and by implication, adult education work carried out in the context of this relationship, might be considered problematic in light of Michael Hardt and Antonio Negri's strong reservations concerning social democratic parties, referred to earlier on in this essay. How far are the policies of the present day PT different from those of the social democratic parties which Hardt and Negri decried? Is there a difference between the PT when operating at the federal level and the same party when operating at the state and municipal levels?

The extended reference to Brazil brings to mind an important education movement which is to be found not only in this large country but throughout Latin America. I am here referring to the Popular Education (Kane, 2001) movement that is a strong popular social movement in Latin America. I would dare say that the Popular Education movement is nowadays an international movement, very strong in North America for instance. Freire is the most heralded popular educator, the chief exponent of the kind of education this movement seeks to promote and therefore one of its key sources of reference. Popular Education, involving non-formal education, finds its natural home in clandestine settings, in revolutionary contexts such as in Nicaragua after 1979 (Arnove, 1986), in Christian Base Communities (CEBs) and, especially as far as First World countries are concerned, in progressive social movements and organizations. One can point, as an example, to a particular Canadian project in Toronto known as the 'naming the moment' project that entails a Gramscian process of 'conjunctural analysis'. This project was carried out at the Jesuit-run Centre for Faith and Justice and the Doris Marshall Institute (see Cavanagh in Borg and Mayo, 2007). The MST engages in popular education and is inspired by Freire (Kane, 2001).

Freire's fascination with and belief in the transformative power of progressive social movements is best captured by his widow and second wife, Anna Maria Araujo Freire, known as Nita Freire, in the following excerpts from an interview my colleague Carmel Borg and I carried out with her in São Paulo in April 1998 (Nita Freire in Borg and Mayo, 2007).

> Nita Freire: Travelling all over this immense Brazil we saw and cooperated with a very large number of social movements of different sizes and natures, but who had (and continue to have) a point in common: the hope in their people's power of transformation. They are teachers – many of them are 'lay': embroiderers, sisters, workers, fishermen, peasants, etc., scattered all over the country, in favelas, camps or houses, men and women with an incredible leadership strength, bound together in small and local organizations, but with such a latent potential that it filled us, Paulo and me, with hope for better days for our people. Many others participated in a more organized way in

> the MST . . . the trade unions, CUT . . . and CEBs: *Christian Base Communities*. As the man of hope he always was, Paulo knew he would not remain alone. Millions of persons, excluded from the system, are struggling in this country, as they free themselves from oppression, to also liberate their oppressors. Paulo died a few days after the arrival of the MST March in Brasília. On that April day, standing in our living-room, seeing on the TV the crowds of men, women and children entering the capital in such an orderly and dignified way, full of emotion, he cried out: 'That's it, Brazilian people, the country belongs to all of us! Let us build together a democratic country, just and happy!' (Nita Freire, in Borg and Mayo, 2007, p. 3)

It is alas common to associate the Brazilian educator's ideas solely with adult literacy education. This does not do justice to Freire's work. His ideas seem relevant to contexts where the participants are 'literate' in the conventional sense of the term. His pedagogical approach focuses on exploring the contradictions concealed by the dominant ideology. This is precisely the task which social justice–oriented social movements carry out, when raising awareness about the issues of oppression with which they are particularly concerned.

Freire's pedagogy recognizes the political nature of all educational activity, where the concern is with doing away with undemocratic social relations and replacing them with radically democratic ones. This is very much the concern of most progressive and social justice–oriented social movements. It is a pedagogy that challenges the bases of 'legitimized' social relations. Many are those who incorporate Freire's thinking in their work and this applies to most radically progressive and social justice–oriented social movements.

Social movements are themselves learning sites (Welton, 1993). There is a learning dimension to their work and that of the organizations they include. One learns through mobilization, awareness raising activities, organizing a campaign, teach-ins, marches, sit-ins or sit-outs, poster sessions and the like. One also learns through participation in a strike – the meaning of solidarity, issues concerning industrial relations, negotiation strategies and so forth. Much learning takes place in social action, as Griff Foley (1999) has so ably documented. Social movements also comprise adult learning organizations, such as workers' education institutions forming part of the labour movement. Adult education is itself often conceived of as a movement. This often takes a specific form: for example the Peace Education movement or the Popular Education movement cited earlier. In the latter case, however, participation extends beyond adults to involve also children, including those having little or no access to schooling. Freire however does not present simply a rosy picture of social movements. He warns against the dangers of co-optation. Social movements can be the target of co-optation strategies when lured into the corporate state sector. Governments, for their part, can pre-empt the emergence of a social movement in a specific area by creating a commission to fill in the void. These commissions would be perceived as being more controllable. Governments seek to ensure stability and normalization of social relations. They would rather deal with bodies whose action is largely predictable. Large, supranational organizations such as the EU can also seek to control the agendas of social movements through their funding structures. This however often turns into a 'cat and mouse' game with organizations belonging to social movements seeking to re-direct EU funds to their progressive ends; often a Gramscian 'war of position' is waged in this context.

This very much applies to the European adult education field where adult education agencies are increasingly becoming dependent on EU funding including the 'employability' oriented ESF (European Social Fund). Belonging to a social movement is crucial for an organization of this kind not to lose sight of its original goals and not to suffer burn-out resulting from the inexorable quest for funds and the excessive paper work and overwhelming administrative tasks involved.

Social movements have often been criticized for the fragmentation they bring about on the Left especially with their focus on single-issue politics. Nawal El Saadawi warns against their being part of a postmodern 'divide and rule' situation, with a unifying globalization from above being challenged by a disruptive fragmentation from below:

> The movement towards a global culture is therefore not contradicted by this postmodern tendency towards cultural fragmentation and identity struggles. They are two faces of the same coin. To unify power, economic power at the top it is necessary to fragment power at the bottom. To maintain the global economy of the few, of the multinationals, unification must exist at the top, amongst the few, the very few. (El Saadawi, 1997, pp. 121–2)

The greatest challenge for adult education is to educate for solidarity without destroying the individual character of movements. After all, the concept of 'movement of movements' is said to be characterized by 'its heterogeneous constituency' (OSAL and CLACSO, 2003, p. 264). Here the question of educating within and for alliances – possibly an enduring Gramscian 'historical bloc' – becomes important and, once again, the finest example here would probably be that provided by the 'movement of movements' connected with the World Social Forum.

Freire spoke about educating for greater coherence, the sort of coherence that can lead to 'greater unity in diversity'. This quest for coherence is crucial to developing the necessary forms of solidarity between people who are different and between the progressive and social justice–oriented movements that represent their interests. The emphasis on the quest for coherence as an ongoing process reflects a recognition, on Freire's part, that forms of domestication, detrimental to others, can emerge from an ostensibly emancipatory practice. The contradictions arising from our multiple and layered subjectivities render this a constant possibility.

Being based on *praxis*, on the recognition of our 'unfinishedness' as human beings and as pedagogues and on the constant need to engage in annunciation and denunciation, genuine adult education, inspired by Freire, involves the ongoing struggle of reflecting on oneself, on the social collectivity involved and on the pedagogical practice. This is done with a view to transformative action – action intended to enable one to confront one's contradictions to become less 'unfinished'/incomplete, less incoherent. This emerges from the piece by Freire in *Mentoring the Mentor* (Freire, 1997) where he replies to a number of authors, in the same book, who took up his ideas. I maintain however that it was always present in his work. It is implied in Freire's exhortation, in *Pedagogy of the Oppressed*, to recognize the presence of and to confront the 'oppressor within' (the 'oppressor consciousness' – the internalization of the oppressor's image).

In this work, Freire had argued that, through a problem-posing approach to education, human beings are conceived of as persons engaged in a 'process of becoming'; they are unfinished persons engaged in and with an 'unfinished reality' (Freire, 1970, 1993, p. 84). Being central to his notion of history as possibility, the notion of 'incompleteness' remains a central theme in his work and features in practically all of his later works. The more complete we become the less contradictory we are in relation to ourselves and others. This is an important step in the direction of engaging in solidarity with others. And social movements have an important role to play in generating the necessary awareness and educational programmes for this purpose. They would enable their adherents to become less incomplete and contradictory and therefore more coherent. And this coherence can help bring people, and movements, together.

LESSONS FROM FREIRE

Finally there are important lessons from Freire that one can heed with respect to providing a liberating education in the context of progressive social movements. People being educated within movements need to have a sense of purpose (as indicated in Chapter 3) – on whose side are we? They also require a critical attitude and should be educated to avoid cynicism in the belief that another world is possible – 'Um outro mundo é possível', to adopt the Porto Alegre 2002 slogan.

Any critique must derive from the existence of an alternative vision of things, a healthy utopia, if you will. It should be the product of an educated sense of hope (see Giroux, 2001, p. 125). The purpose of a critical education on the lines advocated by Freire is to provide greater coherence and this should be an ongoing process.

Furthermore, this process of education underlines the collective dimension of knowledge and learning. For, as Freire stated, time and time again, liberation is not an individual but a *collective* process. Freire argued that one engages in the task of becoming more fully human, the main feature of an education for liberation, not on one's own (it is not an individualistic endeavour) but in solidarity with others (Freire, 1970a, 1993, pp. 85–6). Freire argues, in this context, that, in adopting an individualistic approach to being authentically human, to attaining liberation from oppression, one would be denying others the chance of attaining the same state. Adult education in connection with social movements and carried out on Freirean lines must emphasize the collective dimension of learning and knowledge creation – reading and transforming the world *together*. This approach to adult education would enable us to give meaning to the French revolutionary ideal of 'fraternity', which needs to be recast to capture the equally important notion of sisterhood. It entails

> replacing the relationship of competition, fierce dispute, war of all against all – which, in current society, makes the individual . . . a *homini lupus* (a wolf to other human beings) – with a relationship of cooperation, sharing, mutual help, solidarity. (Löwy and Betto, 2003, p. 334)

These important words by Michael Löwy and the distinguished lay Dominican friar Frei Betto were pronounced in connection with the World Social Forum. They were written in the context of a discussion concerning a genuinely socialist alternative to the world that emerged from the 'Washington Consensus', an alternative in which life-centred values overtake the market driven and therefore predominantly monetary values that are at the heart of the ever increasing attempts to turn all aspects of life into commodities, that fetish to which Karl Marx alerted us more than a century and a half ago. It would seem that a radical adult education, within social movements, and inspired by Freire, of whom Frei Betto claims to be a disciple (Betto in Borg and Mayo, 2007, p. 34), can contribute to the ushering in' of this 'New Civilization', that other world that is possible.

CHAPTER 5

The Competence Discourse and the Struggle for Social Agency and Citizenship: A Freirean Perspective

The discourse concerning education for citizenship is characterized by a struggle over meaning and values. It reflects the struggle over what kind of world we consider possible and the role that people can play in shaping this ever-evolving world. It therefore also involves the struggle over the meaning of education. What purpose should it serve? Put crudely, is it an education intended to integrate persons into the world as we know it, a world in which 'what is' and 'what works' determine what is possible? On the contrary, is it an education that is dynamic and which prepares people for a world not as it is but as it should and can be? The more progressive literature advocates the latter vision and approach. It argues for an education closely connected with a revitalization of the democratic public sphere and which prepares citizens to contribute to the emergence of a 'substantive democracy' (Giroux, 2001). An education for citizenship, in this context, is a democratic education, one in which students learn about democracy not simply by talking about it but by engaging in a democratic learning experience governed by non-hierarchical social relations of education. This is in keeping with John Dewey's over-arching concept of education for democracy.

Alas, this is a far cry from the dominant discourse in education that highlights a 'commercially and market-oriented' type of competence-based learning (Gadotti, 2008, p. 43), competences that are often measured through a positivist approach and according to outcomes. This dominant discourse reflects a broader discourse that promotes entrepreneurship, competitiveness and the mobility of capital and labour in a world characterized by the intensification of globalization.

In several places, the discourse regarding this type of competences originally made its presence strongly felt in the area of vocational education. What is worrying is that this discourse is nowadays not restricted to vocational education. It is a hegemonic discourse that reflects an attempt to render such areas as the education of adults, within the context of the broader all embracing process of lifelong learning, competence and outcomes based. One can detect here the influence of the Organisation for Economic Co-operation and Development (OECD, 1996, 2007) and the European Union (EU), as manifest in the various documents concerning lifelong learning. The 'Memorandum on Lifelong Learning' is a case in point (CEC, 2000). For a variety of reasons, including that of facilitating the harmonization of various national educational systems, *everything has to produce results that can be measured* (Harris, 2007; Landri, 2009; Surian, 2006; Wain, 2004a,b) *in terms of effective outcomes*, a process referred to by Jean Francois Lyotard (1989) as 'performativity' (pp. 47–53). This militates against in-depth interpretative qualitative research processes as everything needs to translate to a quantitative measurement. This is all part and parcel of what has come to be regarded as the 'evaluator state' (Gentili, 2005). The evaluator state exerts control over educational processes through various evaluation schemes, standardization procedures, classifications, outcomes-based funding mechanisms and league tables (CHEPS, 2007, section II; Gentili, 2005, p. 141).

As several writers have shown (Bauman, 2005; Borg and Mayo, 2006; Brine, 1999; Wain, 2004a,b; Williamson, 1998), the dominant competence-based discourse on adult learning, within the context of lifelong learning, focuses on vocational education and ICT. The old UNESCO discourse on lifelong education, to which Ettore Gelpi, Bogdan Suchodolski, Paul Lengrand and others made substantial contributions, and which was based on an expansive and humanist concept of education and human capacities, is reduced to a discourse of learning that serves to project a two-dimensional image of persons, that of producers and consumers.

The kind of competences given importance in the dominant discourse are those that should, in theory, enable persons to become more in demand in the labour market, more 'marketable' as everything seems geared towards an education for 'employability' which, as Ettore Gelpi (2002) reminds us, does not necessarily mean 'employment'. In this context, 'Lifelong Learning', signifies the updating of competences in a vocational sense in view of the 'technological advancement' and potential 'territorial mobility' of capital. Among other functions, the neoliberal state takes on the responsibility of developing the infrastructure that facilitates the mobility of capital. Education, and especially post-compulsory education, including adult education, serves to develop the so-called human resources. Developing human resources signifies, in this context, the attainment of those competences that attract and maintain investment and that permit the labour force to render industry more competitive.

Granted, there is a need for a good vocational adult education set up; nothing wrong here. What is wrong, in my view, is the reduction of what ought to be a broad range of human competences in education to narrowly defined competences, those that fit the labour market and the perceived demands of the economy. Equally worrying is the tendency to promote the idea of education as an individual and not a social responsibility. Jane Thompson, leading UK feminist, socialist educator and activist, who once edited a very influential volume promoting a radical debate on adult education (Thompson, 1980), is on target when she states:

> the advance of individualism and consumerism in western economies, fuelled by the collapse of communism and promoted by neo-liberal governments as emblematic of freedom and democracy, has shifted the focus of attention from the collective and the public towards the individual and the private. As a consequence no one speaks in favour of working class solidarity anymore. Trade unions have been neutralised and professionalised. Feminism as a political movement has been effectively smashed. Black politics has been co-opted by multiculturalism, controlled by institutionalised racism and poverty, and in some respects, pushed towards reactionary forms of fundamentalism. (Thompson, in Borg and Mayo, 2007, p. 65)

This tendency is neoliberal, or more precisely, a concession (a painful one?), by influential but, as always, non-monolithic institutions (e.g. the EU), to the global neoliberal scenario. According to this perspective, individuals are called on to finance wholly or partially their own access to adult education, as though they are purchasing a consumer product rather than availing themselves of a public service to which they are entitled as citizens. This represents the *commodification* of education.

If we are serious about a person's right to education, then we must develop a broader notion of 'competences'. We need a more holistic model of 'competences' if we are to use this hegemonic term and recast it to suit more expansive democratic purposes. Such a holistic model would be more in keeping with the German and Austrian tradition in this area (Sultana, 2009; Winterton et al., 2005) a tradition which, in Germany's case, is closely linked to the concept of *Bildung*. Adopting this alternative model would allow us to develop a repertoire of competences that are open and flexible enough and which would allow persons to develop as subjects exerting an active control over themselves, their existence and their choices in life (Batini, 2008, p. 37). Unfortunately, there is a widening gap between holistic views of education and the needs of the labour market. A new human capital theory approach seems to be making its presence strongly felt. I would argue, however, that the competences required by the labour market can be subsumed within a broader range which also includes the competences for a genuinely active democratic citizenship.

Broadening the notion of 'competences' in this vein, we can speak of competences that enable persons to become, in the words of the Italian critical pedagogue, Lorenzo Milani, to be discussed further on, 'cittadini sovrani' (sovereign citizens). These competences are meant to equip persons not only individually but also collectively, as advocated by Paulo Freire. Persons would thus be equipped with a range of competences that would allow them to contribute to the development of a genuinely democratic environment. A reductionist discourse concerning competences and education would lead to a democratic deficit. It is important to hearken back to the still relevant discourse concerning education, democracy and the public sphere developed by John Dewey, Jurgen Habermas, Aldo Capitini (with his notion of grassroots democracy in a post-fascist Italy – *omnicrazia*), Maxine Greene and others.

In the first of the six key messages in the EU's Memorandum on Lifelong Learning, there is talk of new basic skills, or new literacies, mainly related to work and ICT. The Freirean concept of *critical literacy* is however conspicuous by its absence. Critical literacy entails developing the 'competence' of being able to engage in a critical reading of the world – reading not only the word but also the world. We are here referring to the type of reading in which the students of Lorenzo Milani (Scuola di Barbiana, 1996) were engaged at Barbiana when they read newspapers and discussed articles to which they responded by means of a collective approach to writing. A critical reading of the world would, in my view, constitute the principal competence to develop within an educational process intended to strengthen and regenerate the public sphere – the agora. This can contribute to the development of a kind of democracy often referred to as 'thick democracy' (Gandin and Apple, 2002) that is characterized by direct social participation. I would refer as examples here to the citizenship schools such as those in Porto Alegre that allow persons to acquire the baggage of competences necessary for them to participate directly in the debates concerning the participatory budget (PB). This project is nowadays also being adopted and possibly reinvented in Portugal, Spain (Lucio-Villegas Ramos, 2004; Lucio-Villegas Ramos et al., 2009), France, Italy and Germany while the United Kingdom is going to implement the PB in every municipality from 2012. It is a democratic process in which community members directly decide how to spend part of a public budget (see Sergio Baierle in Borg and Mayo, 2007). With respect to the PB, Daniel Schugurensky states that while many 'local planners, city officials, community organizers and participants do not perceive the pedagogical potential of participatory democracy', a number of 'active participants' in the Porto Alegre project 'understand the Participatory Budget as an educational space', often referring to it as a 'citizenship school' (Schugurensky, 2002, p. 72). He goes on to say, with respect to the PB: 'By engaging actively in deliberation and decision making processes, individuals and communities learn and adopt basic democratic competences and values' (ibid.). A word of caution is however necessary here as many countries and municipalities attempt to adopt a participatory budget. As with Freire's and Milani's ideas, the key word in this context is 'reinvent'. One cannot transplant ideas and projects given the contextually specific characteristics involved. Sergio Baierle, one of the founders of CIDADE, an NGO that carries out research and capacity building with respect to the PB in Porto Alegre, states:

> The Participative Budget is, in a way, the expression of a crisis in local legislative bodies. In my opinion, it is the structural incapacity of these bodies to add and give consequence to demands of the less favored sectors, open a space for the emergence of a fourth power, which is this plebeian public sphere built from the Participative Budget.
>
> The PB is a process and a structure. As a process it cannot be transferred since it comprises our particular history and cannot be cloned. As a structure, although it was built historically and collectively, the Participative Budget can be reinvented elsewhere. Today, in Brazil, even conservative party administrations are implementing forms of Participative Budgets. The World Bank itself has incorporated the idea of PBs as one of its main cores for local development, i.e., if up to a short time ago the neo-liberal policies seemed to consider themselves above more direct social articulations present neo-liberal consensus carries a social project that incorporates the conversion of projects originally presented by the left, through increased scope of space for philanthropic action of great corporations and the search for active consent. That is why the most important discussion may not be as to the possibility of replication, which tends to grow, but as to: What is it good for? Where do we want to arrive? (Baierle, in Borg and Mayo, 2007, pp. 149–51)

One should also think here of social movements engaged in promoting social justice. These movements create the kind of environment which is conducive to the acquisition and learning of various competences. Apart from the various movements that left their mark on the Western world, I would mention such movements as the landless peasant movement (MST) in Brazil, the Chipko movement in India and the Zapatista movement in Chiapas,

Mexico. The competences for active citizenship involved include the ability to mobilize persons around public issues, to develop organizational skills and to exercise rights which would otherwise remain unknown to the persons concerned. They also include the ability to conceive of and create processes of social learning such as methods of non-violent protests, 'teach-ins' and so forth. They also comprise the acquisition of competences for the development of a social solidarity economy. According to the RIPESS (international network for the promotion of the social solidarity economy), this type of economy fosters 'respect for men, women and the environment'.* It returns money to its rightful place, namely as an instrument that facilitates exchanges rather than financial speculation. It is said to pioneer new forms of exchanges.

Social justice–oriented movements are developing a concept of education for citizenship that offers an alternative to the dominant model. The concept also entails use of competences that are given importance in the dominant discourse, for example the use of internet, computers and the like. In this case, however, the competences, which are imparted through an integrated, holistic approach have a social purpose and are considered as vehicles to update strategies and modes of communication. The so-called internet war, engaged in by the Zapatistas, comes to mind. It is a politics of persuasion and mobilization, related to issues concerning the politics of NAFTA, land reform and indigenity, and the right of local communities for autonomy and proper representation in national democratic structures, carried out via electronic networking and information and argumentation on the web.

Nevertheless, another important competence needs to be added to these for a genuine education for active and participatory citizenship, what might be called a 'critical citizenship'. This competence derives from the approach to education developed by

---

*I am indebted to Professor Alessio Surian for this point. See http://lux09.lu/fileadmin/lux09/Newsletter/Lux09-91jours/Charter_of_RIPESS__En_.pdf, accessed on 17 April 2009.

Lorenzo Milani and Paulo Freire: the ability to read critically all that is transmitted via the mass media, including the very same communication and information technologies that are often uncritically celebrated in the dominant discourse. I am convinced that if Louis Althusser were writing today, he would consider the mass media, a major source of 'public pedagogy' (Giroux, 2001), as the principal ideological state apparatus which, as he indicated with regard to all state apparatuses (Althusser, 1971, p. 145), has both its ideological and repressive dimensions. The competence for critical citizenship to be acquired in this context is that of *critical media literacy*:

> Critical media literacy, in our conception, is tied to the project of radical democracy and is concerned to develop skills that will enhance democratization and civic participation. It takes a comprehensive approach that teaches critical skills and how to use media as instruments of social communication and change. The technologies of communication are becoming more and more accessible to young people and ordinary citizens, and can be used to promote education, democratic self-expression, and social justice. (Kellner and Share, 2009, p. 289)

The challenge here is to read not only the word and the world but also the *construction* of the world through the mass media which help shape subjectivities and condition consent for a state of affairs that can prevent people from realizing that another world, a more socially just world, is possible. It also involves, as Douglas Kellner and Jeff Share indicate, the competence to make effective use of the media, to *write* (Taylor, 1993) or *speak* the word and the world, with a view to contributing effectively to the creation of that alternative world that is possible!

CHAPTER 6

Critical Literacy and the Development of a Multi-Ethnic Citizenship: A Freirean Southern-European Perspective

Like all regions of the world, southern Europe and the larger Mediterranean area are under the sway of the phenomenon commonly referred to as globalization, a process that, strictly speaking, has always been a feature of the capitalist mode of production characterized by periodical economic reorganization and an ongoing quest for the exploration of new markets. In fact, it is more appropriate, in the present historical conjuncture, to use the phrase 'the *intensification* of globalization'. This intensification is brought about through developments in the field of information technology. It is a period in which mobility occurs at different levels. There is the constant threat of the 'flight of capital' in a scenario where the process of production is characterized by dispersal and cybernetic control. We also witness the mobility of workers within and beyond the region. People from the south move up north in search of new opportunities.

Migration is an important feature of the Euro-Mediterranean region (Fondazione Laboratorio Mediterraneo, 1997, p. 551). With southern Europe witnessing mass scale immigration from North Africa, the Mediterranean plays an important role in this process, serving, in the view of many, as 'a kind of Rio Grande' (Malabotta, 2002, p. 73).

As a colleague (Carmel Borg) and I have written elsewhere, it can be argued, with respect to the movement of people from the southern Mediterranean to the northern Mediterranean and beyond, that the 'spectre' of the violent colonial process the 'old continent' initiated has come back with a vengeance to 'haunt' it (Borg and Mayo, 2006, p. 45). This process is facilitated by the economic requirements of highly industrialized countries with respect to certain types of labour and the consideration that these requirements cannot be satisfied by the internal labour market, despite the high levels of unemployment experienced within these countries (Apitzsch, 1995, p. 68). This gives rise to the presence of 'guest workers' often the victim of terrible exploitative situations in terms of payment, conditions of work and the precariousness of their existence within the borrowed context. This point was addressed by Paulo Freire who represents a voice from the South that speaks to concerns of the South. In *Pedagogy of Hope*, Freire speaks of his work in Geneva when he came in contact, through meetings and projects, with guest workers from Italy, Spain, Portugal, Greece, Turkey and Arab countries. These migrant guest workers enabled Freire, on his own admission, to begin to come 'in contact with the harsh realities of one the most serious traumas of the "Third World in the First": the reality of the so-called guest workers . . . and their experience of racial, class and sexual discrimination' (Freire, 1994, p. 122). Freire goes on to indicate the fear of the oppressor as one of the challenges to be faced in this context in view of the fact that the opportunity to work, irrespective of how exploitative the conditions are, becomes the primary concern which takes precedence over the concern for political mobilization to confront the exploitation induced by this process of mobility of labour power across national boundaries. This mobility involves, in most cases, a severance from one's roots in view of the process of uneven levels of development that is a characteristic of the capitalist mode of production. Confronting the fear of oppression remains a key challenge here for progressive educators working with migrants; it is a key challenge for progressive educators working in the countries that many of these emigrants left.

Of course the foregoing point applies to most regions in the world and not just the Mediterranean. What renders the whole process significant in the context of this region is, once again, the fact that the receiving countries are the same countries that once witnessed mass waves of emigration. These countries have experienced the shift from being exporters to importers of labour power. This is not the place to engage in a discussion concerning the way the prejudice and racism experienced by settlers from North Africa and elsewhere differs from that experienced in the past by emigrants from today's receiving Mediterranean countries. Nevertheless, in combating xenophobia and racism in this context, one would do well to recall the plight of people from the receiving country when settling abroad or in a more industrially developed region of the same country.

The architectural and demographic landscapes of southern European cities are undergoing significant changes. Against this scenario, we are witnessing the transformation of Mediterranean cities. While the population in these cities increasingly becomes cosmopolitan, the architecture is often a melange of the old co-existing with the new. The global exists alongside the local in a situation of hybridity. Church domes, symbols of Christendom, now stand alongside minarets. This co-existence of architectural symbols of the different monotheistic religions, which have been the subject of much conflict in the past, is becoming an important feature of the skyline of some southern European cities.

Within this cultural hybridity, one can easily encounter the tensions that have characterized the region for centuries. Xenophobia, or more accurately, *islamophobia*, has become widespread. It can be argued that the historical roots for this form of racism can be found, among other things, in the anti-Islamic crusades that left their mark in several places in this region, becoming a feature of their so-called cultural heritage. Cultures that, for centuries, had been constructed as being antagonistic are now expected to co-exist within the same geographical space.

One of the great challenges for educators, in this context, would be that of encouraging participants to cross their mental and cultural borders, to use Henry A. Giroux's (1992) phrase. Crossing borders would, in this context, entail that one begins to understand something about the culture of others, religion included. Perhaps the most important feature of a critical and anti-racist approach to adult education, in this context, is that of developing a process of learning based on authentic dialogue, a key concept in the Freirean pedagogical approach, which is regarded as the means to allow the different cultures in our societies to be an integral feature of the educational process. They would allow participants to listen to others; 'listening' is here being used in the sense conveyed by Paulo Freire in *Pedagogy of Freedom*, where it was argued that 'listening' is to be distinguished from simply 'hearing' and implies one's being 'open to the word of the other, to the gesture of the other, to the differences of the other without being reduced to the other' (Freire, 1998b, p. 107).

The various situations of conflict which characterize this region, and which can cause tension in multi-ethnic societies, render it indispensable that one crosses boundaries in a variety of ways. Many of the southern European regions of the Mediterranean have traditionally been steeped in the Christian religion, mainly Catholic and also Greek Orthodox. In a truly multi-ethnic environment, it is imperative that knowledge of the different religions is provided in adult educational sites and other sites of learning. There is always the danger, however, that one provides a caricature. The complexity of the situation can easily be ignored, with the religions being represented in simplistic terms (Fondazione Laboratorio Mediterraneo, 1997, p. 51).

The study of different religions should therefore be approached with the utmost seriousness and best preparation possible, with special emphasis being placed on the adult educator doing justice to the different religions involved. This applies to adult education carried out in different sites including courses for those involved in the mass media. In the case of the last mentioned, this would be in keeping with the recommendations of the 1997 Civil Forum EuroMed: 'Mass media are invited to present a correct image of religions or cultures resorting, where suitable, to experts on the matter' (Fondazione Laboratorio Mediterraneo, 1997, p. 512).

Misconceptions regarding Islam abound in the Western world. Countries of the north Mediterranean, which are recipients of immigrants from Arab countries, are no exception. For greater conviviality and dialogue to occur between people of different ethnic background with different cultural and related knowledge traditions, an effort must be made to learn about others, to cross the boundaries of one's social location and to obtain the understanding and knowledge necessary to be able to engage in a critical reading of widely diffused texts (media images, news packages, representations in film and documentary) – reading the construction of the world through the word, if I am allowed liberties with Freire's famous phrase. This is necessary for one to be able to confront and problematize (this entails a problem posing approach) the politics of misrepresentation that results from historically entrenched prejudices and deep-seated antagonistic dispositions.

In many countries of southern Europe, we are confronted by a euro-centric cultural heritage that reflects a colonial past, especially in former centres of colonial power such as Spain and Portugal, and, as I mentioned earlier, a past marked by crusades against the Ottoman Empire. A critical approach to adult education in the southern European regions would enable its participants to engage critically with the region's or country's much acclaimed 'cultural heritage' ('culture' not being used in the anthropological sense) and its politics of representation. Exotic and often demonic (mis) representations of 'alterity' abound throughout this cultural heritage, alterity historically having been ascribed, in these areas, to a variety of people, including the 'Saracen' who is regarded as the 'Other' in the context of 'Christian Europe'. The Other becomes the subject of a particular kind of construction, a form of *Orientalism* in Edward Said's sense of the term. This construction denotes a sense of *positional superiority*, also in Said's terms (Said, 1978), on the part of those who promote this particular conception. A critical and Freirean approach to adult education in this region would entail one's engaging critically with the politics of representation underlying different features of the artistic and historical heritage of the various countries in the south European region. A similar politics of representation characterizes the realm of popular culture in the southern European region, with the Sicilian marionette shows, involving Crusaders and the Predator (often the Saracen Other), being a case in point. In introducing immigrants to popular culture traditions in the receiving country, one ought to be wary of the contradictions found within these traditions. They often contain elements that denigrate aspects of the immigrants' own culture.

Cultural productions, at the popular level and at the level of so-called highbrow culture, can serve as codifications, in the sense intended by Paulo Freire. In conceiving of such productions as codifications, we as adult educators would enable ourselves, and those with whom we are working in the educational setting, to engage in a critical reading of our contemporary reality. The concepts that form part of our 'common sense', used in Gramsci's sense of the term, can partly have their roots in our cultural and folklore traditions. Once again, they are concepts that have been accumulated over a long historical period.

I should like to dwell very briefly on one form of cultural production that, in my view, has potential to serve as an educational tool that enables people, from a country that receives immigrants, to empathize with their fellow humans who have arrived from more southern and other shores. Drama is the form of cultural production I have in mind. Drama has been serving as an important educational tool, including a community – learning tool, for several years. The work of Augusto Boal and other cultural workers in various parts of the world, well-documented in the popular education and community studies literature, testifies to this. It has served as a vehicle for the process of codification and decodification, which has been a feature of the Freirean pedagogical approach, although one should be wary not to make a fetish out of it. I would submit, however, that drama can serve as a powerful pedagogical tool to foster greater inter-ethnic solidarity and understanding. I found quite instructive, in this regard, a dramatic representation to which participants at a 1998 conference on education in the Mediterranean held in Sestri Levante, Liguria, Italy, were exposed (Mayo, 2004). It was carried out by a troupe of players from Genoa and involved a juxtaposition of situations concerning the harsh realities of migration, both past and present. The plight of Italians migrating to the United States, Argentina and elsewhere, and of Italians from the south moving into the country's northern regions, was juxtaposed against that of Africans (including Arabs) and Eastern Europeans, with their personal narratives, moving into Italy. The scenes were poignant and quite revealing, based on a dialectical movement between past (a kind of 'redemptive remembrance') and present in the hope of a transformed and healthy multi-ethnic democracy.

To conclude, I would identify the following from among the many challenges to be faced by critical educators in the southern European region to help develop a strong democratic citizenship in a multi-ethnic context:

- Educators should not regard incoming migrant groups as 'deficits'; the programmes and experiences provided should be those in which the members of all ethnic groups involved, including the ethnic groups to which the educators belong, are conceived of as 'subjects' and not as 'objects' in Freire's sense of the terms.

- Educators and policy makers should avoid developing programmes that smack of what the Italians call *assistenzialismo* (a term frequently used by Freire that is often given a literal translation in the English language texts) that often results in a form of 'learned helplessness'.
- Critical educators should be wary of not misrepresenting those constructed, as part of the hegemonic Western discourse, as 'other'.
- Critical educators require a good understanding of political economy and knowledge of how the economic system segregates on ethnic lines. Critical educators need to become 'border crossers': they need to begin to understand something about the culture of others, religion included.
- Critical educators in receiving countries need to recognize the contribution of others to the development of their own culture; this would include recognition of the contribution of non-European cultures to the development of aspects of what is termed 'Western civilisation' (see Elsheikh, 1999, on this and the related issue of the 'debtor's syndrome').
- The pedagogical approach should be one based on the key concept in Freire's work and that of others (e.g. Buber), namely Dialogue that entails listening and not mere hearing.
- Critical educators must recognize that being a migrant constitutes only one aspect of the person's multiple subjectivities and the culture of origin intersects with a variety of other cultures that emerge from other aspects of the person's identity, namely cultures related to gender, class, 'race'/ethnicity, sexuality, age, religion; the term multiculturalism, as I use it, is meant to capture the various cultures that characterized peoples identities and societies in general and should not be used, as seems to be the case in many parts of Europe, interchangeably with multi-ethnicity.

- A critical education would be based on the recognition that, although the work factor weighs heavily on the minds of those who migrate, the notion of citizenship ascribed to them should not be a two-dimensional one, that of producer and consumer, but one in which they are conceived, as with all citizens in a multicultural democracy, as social actors.
- One other point which would draw on Freire's work as education secretary in São Paulo and more recent experiences in Porto Alegre, Ro Grande do Sul, is that schools should not remain isolated from the rest of the community but should be an integral part of this community and their surrounding contexts conceived of in all their multi-ethnic, multicultural and bio-diversity; schools should therefore begin to be developed as multipurpose community learning sites with implications for curricula (covering conventional hours and after hours programmes), administration, teacher/adult educator formation and school architecture; migrants and other groups within the community should be able to feel a sense of ownership of and belonging to the school that would appeal to their children and their own frameworks of relevance both during conventional school hours and after school hours (where physical adjustments need to be made for the creation of spaces that accommodate adults).

I had addressed this theme in an earlier publication (Mayo, 2004, 2010), and I frequently return to it given that it provides the context for my work as a critical educator inspired by Freire among other authors. It raises several issues which will be tackled later in this volume, not least the theme of bicultural education which appears in the chapter on the work of Antonia Darder. Her work is of great relevance to the kind of issues addressed in this chapter.

CHAPTER 7

Popular Education and Transformative Research

Freire's central concept of praxis has ramifications for the more progressive and social justice–oriented popular education. According to this conception, there should be no dichotomy between theoretical rumination and research, each emerging from reflection over the area of action with a view to improving such action to contribute to and foster a more socially just environment. *Pedagogy of the Oppressed* is itself an exemplar of this combination of theory, as a codification of experience, and practice. While not the product of research carried out in a systematic way, and more a reflex on experience, with constant resort to a sophisticated level of theory and historical insight, this and other work by Freire of the same period incorporates excerpts from taped interviews with peasants, even though these are few and far between. The text however is a standard reference for the kind of research intended to contribute towards the transformation of communities and to deepen one's insights into the politics of knowledge.

I would like to state at the outset that books such as this one have served to stimulate my imagination for teaching and grassroots engagement in specific contexts much more than any manual can. I have in mind manuals providing 'mix and stir' recipes. I might be biased here since I come from what was once known as the Foundations of Education. It is also a truism that any research or writing of this kind does not present itself as value free – no research is – and therefore the researcher makes the adopted theoretical perspective known at the outset. More than anything else, this book remains true to its central concept, a pedagogy of praxis. The theory helps the author reflect on his field of practice, a field spanning contexts such as Brazil and Chile. Freire's later work focuses on a much larger field, which comprises Africa, Europe and other parts of Latin America, a number of which were engaged with, as we have seen, during a lengthy period of exile.

The other point that emerges from this and other texts by Freire is the importance of researching the community in which one engages as knowledge worker or cultural worker more generally. This is a key component of the Freirean approach. Popular educators together with learners themselves and other significant resource persons (depending on contexts) are to spend time in the community beforehand, visiting popular places, possibly even visiting houses and so on. The attempt is to gain access to the people's universe of knowledge, including their vocabulary and speech patterns. They had to engage in 'an arduous search for generative words' at the level of 'syllabic richness' and high 'experiential involvement' (Goulet, 1973, p. 11). More generally one can develop a checklist of points and information for research of this kind. My colleague Carmel Borg and I developed such a checklist which could be of use to students in our teacher education programme. These are intended to enable students to research the community in which they will be teaching in order to draw up a community profile. This is still a preliminary attempt that is subject to refinement and retooling.

Perhaps, it must be said, one potential flaw of work involving the educators themselves, including action research, would be the tendency to be less critical of one's practice and too much on the defensive when facing criticisms from outside. The case of Freire and the Guinea Bissau (Freire, 1978) experience comes to mind (see Freire and Faundez, 1989). There is also the danger of rationalization with regard to things that go awry. And certain theoretical insights can be availed of (or abused of) in this regard. I recommend that the reading of transformative accounts and research by the participants themselves should be complemented by the reading of accounts of the same project provided by external observers. Once again, a reader does well to complement her or his reading of the *Cartas* from Guinea Bissau (Freire, 1978) with say the work of Linda Harasim (1983) in a PhD thesis, extensively drawn upon by Freire arch-critic, Blanca Facundo, which sheds more critical light on the Guinea Bissau experience. One can then follow this up by reading Freire's defence of his position in *Reading the World and the World* (Freire and Macedo, 1987).

Freire's work has inspired a number of research projects predicated on praxis, most notably Kirkwood and Kirkwood's (1989) classic text on the Adult Learning Project in Edinburgh, an account that has recently been reprinted and updated (Kirkwood and Kirkwood, 2011). It provides a balanced view, including criticisms, of a much lauded attempt to *reinvent* Freire in a working class context in the Scottish capital. Freire's work has also helped inspire some magnificent forms of action research, through which practitioners in adult education, dissatisfied with the results and relevance of research findings, 'have taken matters into their own hands by conducting their own enquiries focused on finding answers to practical questions' (Kerka, 2005, p. 558). It also inspired other types of qualitative research such as O'Cadiz, Wong and Torres' work on the educational reforms introduced by the Freire-led Educational Secretariat in São Paulo in the late 1980s. This volume brings together theory, political economy and analysis of ethnographic work in the form of interviews with actors in the entire project. This project comprised schooling, involving elements derived from popular education (the 'popular public school') and adult education – *Movimento de Alfabetização de Adultos e Jovens* (MOVA-SP).

This study provides insights by protagonists, policy makers, social movement activists, educators, learners and others with regard to the relationship between say research into 'thematic complexes' (generative themes) from the community and popular education (which, in this context, also comprises 'popular public' schooling) and, to give one example, the relationship between social movements and the state, the latter being most relevant to adult education of the popular education type (MOVA-SP).

The book shuttles from theory to an analysis of practice, providing a fine discussion regarding theories of the state and then dwelling, at considerable length, on the role of social movements in the struggle for power, with specific reference to Latin American social movements. The authors also provide a highly illuminating account of state–social movement relationships in Brazil and the kind of relationships the Freire secretariat sought to establish with respect to the process of educational reform in São Paulo. I consider this to be one of the most important discussions in the book that dwells on transformative education being carried out in the context of broader social movements. The study also conveys the idea that those engaged in the desired process of curriculum reform can constitute a social movement. The theme of being 'strategically outside and tactically inside' or in concert with the state emerges. In short, this type of research, which can be regarded as transformative research, is to be applauded for its combination of macro-, meso- and micro-level discussions. Theory is combined with reproductions from field notes and excerpts from transcribed interviews to provide an honest account of the strengths and limitations of this approach. And while one might question the usefulness of this book for popular education, given that much of it, apart from the MOVA-SP sections, focuses on schools, one needs to underline the adoption of the popular education approach within a reformed schooling context. The study concerns a comprehensive educational reform predicated on some of the accepted Freirean principles of popular education.

Freire's work also helped inspire that innovative approach to community research known as Participatory Action Research (PAR). It was not the only source of inspiration here but this type of research (PAR) embodies some of Freire's insights. Prominent here is the work of the Indian Rajesh Tandon, the Tanzanian Yusuf Kassam, the late Colombian Orlando Fals Borda, the North Americans Budd L Hall and Peter Park (Park et al., 1993) and, as far as critique goes, the recently deceased Mexican Pablo Latapí. In his critique, Latapí provides a nuanced account of PAR. The writings of Rajesh Tandon reflect in many ways the strong tradition of grassroots and often anti-colonial and ecologically sensitive organizing that exists in India (Tandon, 2000a,b; 2003) and his contributions, in this regard, are in keeping with his conception of an alternative development paradigm.

PAR constitutes a form of research that is grassroots oriented, focuses on community problems and issues perceived by the community members to be directly affecting their lives and is carried out by the community members themselves. 'It is a bottom up partnership approach to research and development and rests on the principle that real change (worthwhile, mutually acceptable and sustainable change) occurs only when and if the people concerned are enabled to be inside of the research process' (Obilade, 2005, p. 461). An exclusive association with the type of education deriving from Freire and other Latin America experiences has often led to controversy since there are those who also trace the origins of this approach to Mao and communist China, Islamic groups with a social message and liberation theologians (ibid.). The 'Third World' and 'southern' orientation of all these elements probably explains the convergence of the adopted approaches. Experiments of PAR can be found in a variety of countries. In a lecturing visit to Seville, I was invited to engage with adult learners involved in recuperating personal and collective memories of the Spanish Civil War and the Franco years in a project of this kind. PAR, by its very nature, constitutes a very important form of transformative adult education. People are gathering and producing knowledge at the same time, often experiencing, in the process, what Jack Mezirow would regard as a 'perspective transformation'. Needless to say, there has been much debate with regard to its credibility as an approach to research (Latapí, 1988) but then such debates occur with respect to any form of learning and research that falls outside the mainstream. It would occur with all sorts of research and knowledge *by*, *from* and *about* people on the margins. Like indigenous knowledge, PAR challenges received wisdom and constituted authority.

One other classic narrative which I consider to be of use for transformative research, with implications for popular education, even though it focused on a critique of public schooling and the possibilities offered by an alternative community-based form of collective learning, is the School of Barbiana's *Letter to a Teacher* (Borg et al., 2009), to be discussed later on in comparison with Freire's ideas. This narrative provides a combination of qualitative (vignettes) and quantitative methods (award winning statistical enquiry). The idea of creating vignettes depicting everyday situations is a useful one and this text is instructive in this regard. We also come across this technique in the writing of Mike Newman in such works as *Mailer's Regard* (Newman, 1999, 2002, 2007). And a Maltese researcher, Joseph Vella (1996), used this technique in his research on prison education because of the difficulties encountered with the prison authorities in engaging in more conventional qualitative research involving ethnographic field notes and taped interviews. The vignettes, in the *Letter to a Teacher*, focus on the images of Gianni, the failed working class or peasant class boy in the public school system and Pierino, the middle class boy who becomes part of the ruling class, the 'figli di papa' (daddy's children). Vignettes have always constituted an important technique in social documentation. One can go back to Middle English literature to come across techniques of this kind, *Piers Plowman*, attributed to William Langland, constituting an important example. The connection with Freire lies in the convergence between his approach to education and its dissemination and that encouraged by Lorenzo Milani and his students at Barbiana and at San Donato di Calenzano, the latter being youths and adults. This convergence is highlighted in a recently published piece of mine (Mayo, 2007). Furthermore, *Letter to a Teacher*, which juxtaposes a critique of mainstream selective education with the experiences developed at Barbiana, in a non-formal setting which invites parallels with that of popular education, is written in the form of a reflective narrative, highlighting a particular standpoint, the standpoint of outcasts of the Italian public schooling system. That it is transformative is highlighted by the impact it has had on the 68 movement in Italy, progressive thinking in education in this peninsula and beyond, the Leftist Catholic movement in the same country and some of the leading Italian Left wing intellectuals such as Pier Paolo Pasolini. Pasolini is on record as having stated, in a television documentary produced by *Rai*, the Italian state broadcasting station, that this was one of the few books which captured his imagination at the time.

Narrative is an important feature of transformative research and is promoted by feminists (see, for instance, Ledwith, 2010) and other progressive educators/cultural workers and researchers worldwide (once again, Newman, 1999, 2002, 2007). The connection with Freire can at best be found in Margaret Ledwith's *Community Development. A Critical Approach* (Ledwith, 2005) and Antonia Darder's (2002) *Reinventing Paulo Freire. A Pedagogy of Love.* It is evident from the outset that these books provide no dichotomy between theory and practice but are concerned with *praxis* throughout. Theoretical insights from Freire are elaborated in light of the personal everyday experiences. In Ledwith's book, one finds throughout references to personal narratives anchored in the ordinary and every day. These lives are considered political. The author came across some of the persons involved during her experience as community organizer at Hattersley, Greater Manchester, England. The book, which is theoretically sophisticated, drawing on Gramsci, Freire, Alinksy and others (e.g. Marjorie Mayo, Janet Kenway, Magda Lewis, Chet Bowers and Vandana Shiva) also provides insights from emancipatory (or transformative) action research.

Antonia Darder is, in my estimation, one of the finest exponents of critical pedagogy and I am dedicating a chapter to her. The voices of progressive teachers are reproduced in Darder's work, which ends with a long final chapter consisting of first person narratives by various educators of different class, ethnic and gender backgrounds. Similar narratives with public intellectuals, including popular educators, are found in another book, one with which I have been involved, namely a book of interviews (Borg and Mayo, 2007). It remains a bone of contention as to whether these interviews or narratives should be left to speak for themselves, as they are in the Darder and Borg and Mayo books, or else become the subject of some critical inquiry, as in the case of narrative inquiry (see, for instance, Ledwith, 2005, 2010; Riley and Hawe, 2004; Webster and Mertova, 2007), into the themes raised by these narratives and the lifeworlds they reflect.

I should like to end with a consideration of a possible university research scenario concerning popular education opening up in front of us, as a result of the emerging EU policy discourse. In the first place, there is a widespread concern with the evaluation of narrowly defined competences and their indicators, so called quality indicators, which fits nicely with what Lyotard (1989) calls 'performativity' and which seems to exclude any kind of interpretative enquiry into the critical dimensions of teaching and learning, including adult learning. There are so many aspects of adult learning that cannot be researched by means of narrowly defined competences and their indicators and for which an interpretative approach, which captures the complexity of the situation at hand, without any generalizations, is warranted. Alas this kind of approach, which might well involve 'learning-setting ethnography', akin to 'classroom ethnography' with regard to schooling, and in-depth interviewing, including focus group interviews, is hardly given any consideration in the EU discourse on adult learning and lifelong learning more generally. This militates against the kind of approach which I consider necessary to capture the dynamics of a Freirean dialogical approach to popular education. Secondly, we have an emerging and dominant discourse about higher education which, apart from being strictly vocational and technical-rational in scope, centring around employability (which does not mean employment, Gelpi, 2002) and ICT, focuses on diversification and competitiveness (Mayo, 2009b). The concern with diversification in the organization of higher education has strong ramifications for university research that is community oriented and meant to be socially transformative. Some institutions are meant to be 'big league' players serving as world class research institutions, some are meant to be purely teaching institutions while others are meant to have a regional focus, that is, to gear their teaching and research to regional development needs. The EC communiqué of 2006 states explicitly that not all institutions need to strike the same balance between education and research (CEC, 2003, p. 18; 2006, 4). The then commissioner in the area, Jan Figel, was however less prudent in the way he made the same point:

> the huge levels of research funding [*in the USA*] are overwhelming[*ly*] concentrated on around 100 research intensive universities and fewer than 250 institutions award post-graduate degrees . . . Europe's universities should be allowed to diversify and specialise: some must be able to play in the major league, but others should concentrate on regional or local needs and perhaps more on teaching. (Figel, 2006, p. 7)

A number of interrelated questions arise. Will this mean that there will be an attempt to confine cutting edge adult and popular education research to 'premier league' universities, community oriented work to local and regional development universities and adult educator or popular educator preparation programmes to 'teaching' universities? Would not such a separation of tasks be detrimental to the quality of each component? Would it not undermine the notion of praxis in transformative research in popular education?

CHAPTER 8

Adult Learning, Teaching and Programme Planning: Insights from Freire

In this chapter, I shall revisit some of the concepts outlined earlier (Chapter 2) and see how they fit the mundane but nevertheless important domain of programme planning and guidelines for pedagogical encounters in learning settings. My focus is specifically on adult learning settings but I write this chapter in the hope that the ideas resonate with the needs and critical pedagogical aspirations of those involved in other settings, including school settings (Freire adopted and reinvented many of his ideas with respect to the development of popular public schools in São Paulo when he served as education secretary there) and higher education settings.

KNOWLEDGE OF THE COMMUNITY

Freire's pedagogy emerged from the Latin American tradition of popular education, which incorporates a strong degree of non-formal education. Non-formal education is not *laissez faire* pedagogy but includes a certain degree of planning and organization. In the classic Freirean approach, the entire process of planning involves an intimate knowledge of the community in which the learning is to take place. The team of educators and project organizers, and other project participants, were allowed to mix with community members in a variety of settings, including their most informal settings, listen to their speech patterns and concerns as well as identify some of the thematic complexes of the community itself. This approach, as already indicated, was repeated and reinvented by Freire within the context of public educational administration when he served as educational secretary in the Municipal Government of São Paulo in his native Brazil (O'Cadiz et al., 1998).

CODIFICATION

Once the information was gathered, the team worked together and consulted community members, besides other persons connected with the locality, to draw up a plan of action that focused on the 'reality' gleaned from the research carried out in the locality. Important aspects of this reality were thus codified in the form of pictures, subjects for discussion, plays, generative themes and other pedagogical approaches. The material connected with the participants' framework of relevance but was codified in such a way that it allowed the participants to gain some critical distance from the matter being discussed. This process of gaining critical distance is what *praxis* is all about. By now it will be clear that praxis is the central concept in Freire's pedagogy.

Recall that it involves reflection upon action for transformative learning and action. This is how Freire defines praxis in *Pedagogy of the Oppressed*.

> But human activity consists of action and reflection: it is praxis, it is transformation of the world. (Freire, 1970a, 1993, p. 125)

EXILE AS PRAXIS

Freire goes on to say that the whole process involved needs to be enlightened through theory. Freire and other intellectuals, with whom he has conversed in 'talking books', conceive of different learning situations in their life as forms of praxis. This applies to adult learning in its broadest contexts including learning from life situations – informal learning. These situations are viewed as moments when people can gain critical distance from the context they know to perceive it in a more critical light. For instance, Freire and the Chilean Antonio Faundez (Freire and Faundez, 1989) considered exile a form of praxis. Freire makes statements to this effect also in a book with Ricardo Kotscho and Frei Betto (Betto and Freire, 1986). He refers to the period of exile as one that provided a profoundly pedagogical experience, thus echoing Frei Betto who also presented, in the same discussion, his 4-year experience of imprisonment, under the military dictatorship, as one that had a strong and important pedagogical dimension. Freire's period of exile is presented as a time during which he gained distance from Brazil and began to understand himself and Brazil better. It was a case of obtaining distance from what he had carried out in Brazil to prepare himself better to continue being active outside his context.

ANTITHESIS OF PRAXIS: EMPTY THEORIZING AND MINDLESS ACTIVISM

Freire relates the whole process of action and reflection to theory and practice (Betto and Freire, 1986). Freire's underscores the point that action on its own, isolated from reflection, constitutes mindless activism. Likewise, reflection on its own, divorced from action, constitutes empty theorizing. It is for this reason that Freire, in keeping with the Marxist tradition, regards one's material surroundings as the basis for the development of one's consciousness. In the words of Marx and Engels: 'Consciousness is, therefore, from the beginning a social product, and remains so as long as men (*sic*) exist at all' (Marx and Engels, 1970, p. 51). The notion of praxis that lies at the heart of Freire's pedagogical approach and which informs learning contexts developed on Freirean lines is akin to Marx and Engels' notion of 'revolutionizing practice' as expressed in the *Theses on Feuerbach*.

DIALECTICAL RELATIONS

The 'action-reflection–transformative action', process is dialectical (Allman, 1999, 2001). In the introduction to the special issue of *Convergence* dedicated to Freire, Allman et al. (1998) state:

> Dialectical thinkers understand the internal relations among all phenomena. In the case of human beings or groups, this is a social relation which could be harmonious but which, thus far in history, normally has been antagonistic, resulting in various social relations that Freire collectively refers to as the oppressor-oppressed relation (e.g. class relations, gender, race, colonial, etc.) The antagonism is often so great that nothing short of abolishing the dialectical relation will improve the situation. When there are no longer the two opposing groups, the possibility emerges of human beings uniting in love, with a commitment to social justice and to care for all of our social and natural world. (p. 10)

TEACHER–STUDENT AND STUDENTS–TEACHERS

Learners can be assisted in this process of praxis, of coming to understand their reality in a more critical light, through a process of what Freire calls authentic dialogue and participatory learning, as well as collective learning. The educator learns from the learners in the same way that the latter learn from her or him, the roles of educator and learner becoming almost interchangeable. In what has become a classic formulation, Freire wrote about 'teacher–student' and 'students–teachers'. The educator is therefore regarded as a person who, while engaging in dialogue with the learners, is also being taught by them. The learners, for their part, are also teaching while being taught (Freire, 1970a, 1993, p. 80). In a dialogue with Ira Shor, Freire states:

> Liberatory education is fundamentally a situation where the teacher and the students *both* have to be learners, *both* have to be cognitive subjects, in spite of their being different. This for me is the first test of liberating education, for teachers and students both to be critical agents in the act of knowing. (Freire, in Shor and Freire, 1987, p. 33)

LEARNER AS SUBJECT

The educator would therefore transcend the boundaries of his/her social location to understand and act in solidarity with the learners, no longer perceived as 'Other'. In adopting a Freirean approach, one would regard educators and learners as subjects in a humanizing relationship. Solidarity is the hallmark of this pedagogical relationship. The learner's reality constitutes an integral part of the subject matter that, therefore, becomes a mediator between the two subjects in question, that is educator and learner. Freire goes on to state that the dialogical process of education marks 'the sealing together of the teacher and the students in the joint act of knowing and re-knowing the object' (Shor and Freire, 1987, p. 100). Borrowing from this conversation between Freire and Shor, one can argue that anything that the educator already knows is relearned when studied again with the learners, a point confirmed by Freire in the same conversation (ibid.).

LEARNERS AND EDUCATORS NOT EQUAL

However, and here comes the apparent contradiction, a Freirean approach to learning based on dialogue is one wherein educators and learners are not on an equal footing.

> Obviously, we also have to underscore that while we recognize that we have to learn from our students . . . this does not mean that teachers and students are the same . . . there is a difference between the educator and the student. (Freire, 1985, p. 177)

Much depends on the specific situation in which the adult learning process occurs but it would be amiss to celebrate learner voices uncritically, since they are never innocent (Aronowitz and Giroux, 1991, pp.130–1). They contain various manifestations of the 'oppressor consciousness' which ought to be challenged. Dialogue, as conceived of by Freire, also involves educators allowing themselves to be challenged and also to constantly undergo self-reflection and scrutiny to confront the 'oppressor consciousness' within. In short, both educator and learner need to address their contradictions in an ongoing process of gaining greater coherence. The educator needs to help create the conditions whereby the learners develop the confidence necessary to challenge him or her where necessary in a situation of mutual respect and trust. This is part of the humility which, according to Freire, all critical educators must show.

DIRECTIVE APPROACH

The *directive* nature of the educational process is affirmed (see, for instance, the discussion with Moacir Gadotti and Sergio Guimarães published in Brazil in 1989 – Freire, in Gadotti et al., 1995, p. 50). Guarding against the perceived danger of a *laissez-faire* pedagogy, resulting from a misconception of his particular notion of dialogue, Freire emphasizes this directivity in the conversation with Ira Shor and elsewhere: 'At the moment the teacher begins the dialogue, he or she knows a great deal, first in terms of knowledge and second in terms of the horizon that he or she wants to get to. The starting point is what the teacher knows about the object and where the teacher wants to go with it' (Freire, in Shor and Freire, 1987, p. 103).

Freire makes it clear that he believes that the educators' pedagogical action is guided by a particular political vision and theoretical understanding. Freire, after all, considers education to be a political act, there being no such thing as a neutral education, with educators having to answer the question 'for whom and on whose behalf they are working' (Freire, 1985, p. 180). Freire once stated that the learning experience entails a process of research and curiosity with all the elements involved – teacher, student, knowing object, methods, techniques – providing direction (Freire, in Fabbri and Gomes, 1995, p. 96). He argues that it is for this reason that every form of educational practice is directive but not necessarily manipulative and that every educational practice cannot be neutral; a directive practice cannot be neutral – no one is neutral when facing an objective to be reached (ibid.).

AUTHORITY AND AUTHORITARIANISM

Educators therefore have a directive role; they need to exercise their authority, an authority derived from their competence as pedagogues. We have seen however how Freire drew an important distinction between *authority* and *authoritarianism*. It is imperative that the authority derived from one's pedagogical competence does not degenerate into authoritarianism: 'the democratic teacher never, never transforms authority into authoritarianism' (Freire, in Shor and Freire, 1987, p. 91). This authoritarianism would render the difference that exists between educator and learner 'antagonistic' (Freire, in Gadotti et al., 1995, p. 50). The educator exercises what Ira Shor calls 'democratic authority' (Shor, 1992, pp. 156–8).

What we have therefore in Freire's nuanced concept of dialogue is a paradox rather than a contradiction. Freire provides a complex notion of learning and instruction, based on dialogue. Freire (1974) feels that the traditional educator regards the knowledge he or she possesses, often captured in the lesson plan, as 'complete'. The Freirean inspired educator regards knowledge as dynamic, an object of co-investigation and unveiling that necessitates the participation of co-knowing subjects – the learners. The process of knowing involved, with respect to the object of knowledge, is considered by both educator and learner as 'incomplete' (see Allman, 2001).

TACT AND PRUDENCE

Freire has even advocated tact and prudence when engaging in a dialogical approach, conceding that people who have been conditioned by many years of exposure to 'banking education' do not immediately do away with this conditioning to embrace dialogue. They often resist attempts at dialogue, perhaps even misconstruing a dialogical approach for lack of competence on the educator's part. Freire concedes that some instruction is necessary at times. It is for this reason that he once stated that an educator can alternate between traditional and progressive teaching. It is as though he seems to be saying that, in such difficult circumstances, dialogue should be introduced only gradually (see Horton and Freire, 1990, p. 160). Elements of the 'old' pedagogy can co-exist with the new in an overall context that however privileges democratic relations.

Given the strong relationship between knowledge and the learner's existential situation in Freire's approach, one assumes that the participant has a repository to draw on. This repository consists of one's life experience. The participant is therefore encouraged to draw on this experience in order to arrive at new knowledge, at a new awareness. In drawing on this experience, one is able to relate to the codified material. The educator enables this process to occur not by 'depositing' knowledge but by engaging the learner's critical faculties. Rather than being a dispenser of knowledge, the educator poses questions, problematizes issues. In this problem-posing education, the pedagogy applied is primarily not that of 'the answer' but that of 'the question' (Bruss and Macedo, 1985).

COLLECTIVE DIMENSIONS OF LEARNING

In adopting a democratic, dialogical approach, the circle or learning setting serves as a microcosm indicating the potential that can exist within contexts characterized by democratic social relations. Furthermore, knowledge itself is democratized and is therefore not presented any longer as the preserve of a privileged minority. Furthermore, the knowledge disseminated is in itself 'democratic' in that its starting point is the life experienced by the participants and serves their interests. Finally, it is group knowledge that emerges from this experience that emphasizes the *collective* dimensions of learning and of action for social change. Freire argued that one engages in the task of becoming 'more fully human' not on one's own (it is not an individualistic endeavour) but in solidarity with others (Freire, 1970a, 1993, pp. 85–6). This having been said, one eventually moves beyond the 'here and now' to gain a greater level of awareness. 'Educands' concrete localization is the point of departure for the knowledge they create of the world' (Freire, 1994, p. 85). It is just the point of departure. For the 'here and now' represents only the starting point of an ongoing adult learning process and not the end point. Remaining within the here and now constitutes, according to Freire, a case of populism or *basismo*. In remaining there and not moving beyond (through co-investigation of the object of inquiry), one would be engaging in 'basism', the romanticization (or 'mythification') of the vernacular (see Freire, 1994, p. 84).

It is this aspect of a Freire inspired theory of instruction, learning and curriculum planning that renders it quite different from the more liberal notion of learning through dialogue which often erroneously passes off as 'Freirean'.

The insights we derive from Freire, with regard to programme planning, learning and instruction in adult education, are the following.

Planning together

One should not enter the community and impose a programme on its members but should, on the contrary, engage with a team of researchers, preferably including people with different disciplinary backgrounds and certainly including both educators and potential project participants (the adult learners), in studying the community, where the learning setting is to be developed, at close hand. This process of study or research comprises informal meetings with community members. The planning of materials occurs on the basis of the insights and information gleaned from the research.

Learning and instruction

Learning based on action and reflection

The approach throughout is one based on *praxis* involving critical reflection on the area of action which also involves recourse to theory but which entails an authentic notion of dialogue in which the subject of enquiry is the focus of collective co-investigation. The research leads to insights which are to form the basis of the codified learning material whereby the educator enables the learners to gain critical distance from the community they know to be able to perceive it in a different, hopefully more critical light. The same applies to the adult educator herself or himself who also gains critical distance from the object of co-investigation and can come to perceive it in a more critical light. We have seen how even exile is seen by Freire and co-authors, engaged in dialogue with him, as a form of praxis, of gaining critical distance.

Adult educators working with migrants in this ever growing context for adult education can take a leaf out of Freire's book. One of the challenges for critical pedagogical work with migrants, to emerge from this Freirean insight, is that of enabling the migrants to read not only the world they now inhabit as immigrants but also the world they left through a process of obtaining critical distance from their context of origin. This can hopefully lead to a greater understanding of the politics of their own dislocation.

Dynamic knowledge

Through this process of praxis, based on reflection on action, knowledge is conceived of as dynamic rather than static. The approach to learning is *directive* since learning is conceived of as a political act. The roles of adult educator and adult learner are almost interchangeable, as all learn from each other, but this is not to say that the adult learner and adult educator are on an equal footing. The latter must have a certain amount of authority which should not be allowed to degenerate into authoritarianism lest the spirit of genuine dialogue would be destroyed.

Starting with the learners' existential realities

Only through dialogue does the group learn collectively to unveil the contradictions that underlie the reality on which it is focusing. Adult educators are encouraged to show tact when promoting dialogical relations and there are moments when they temper dialogue with a certain degree of instruction, especially on consideration that people exposed for years to banking education do not embrace dialogue easily. As indicated earlier, however, one starts from the learners' existential reality without remaining at that level. Adult educators must demonstrate the humility necessary to be disposed to relearn that which they think they already know through their dialogic interactions with the rest of the learning group or community.

AFFINITIES WITH FREIRE

CHAPTER 9

Paulo Freire and Lorenzo Milani

Lorenzo Milani (1923–67) and Paulo Freire (1921–97) are widely regarded as two figures who can provide insights for a critical approach to education. Milani is certainly revered in southern Europe, especially his native Italy, for his radical approach to education and schooling in particular. He has gained recognition in the English speaking world since some of the works he wrote (those concerning his trial and tribulations) and others with which he is strongly associated (*Lettera a Una Professoressa – Letter to a Teacher*) have been translated into English and have been the subject of some insightful discussions. The *Lettera a Una Professoressa* (henceforth the *Lettera*) has also been translated into Spanish and read in Freire's Latin America, albeit clandestinely in those countries that went through fascist dictatorial periods. Milani is less known than Freire in critical education circles and it is only recently that he is being considered as a potential international contributor to that area known as critical pedagogy (Borg and Mayo, 2006). This essay will highlight the common elements, as well as divergences, in both that can help educators adopt a critical approach to education, an approach that is predicated on social justice and that therefore signifies an option for the oppressed.

One would feel inclined to ask: why bother to provide a comparative study of the ideas of these two figures? What is there to be had from such an exercise? My view is that despite the differences in geographical contexts and the periods in which they lived and worked, there is so much convergence between the two, including their democratic Left leaning approach to education, not to mention the radical social justice–oriented religious influence felt in both, that they together provide nourishment for those seeking insights and pedagogical signposts for a truly social justice education. It is with this intention in mind that I engage in this comparative exercise, hoping to provide a brief attempt at a synthesis towards the end. I start off by introducing Lorenzo Milani to those not familiar with his biography, drawing on the authoritative biographical accounts provided by the late Neera Fallaci (Fallaci, 1993), sister of the more famous and also late O riana Fallaci, and Giorgio Pecorini (1998).

LORENZO MILANI (1923–67)

Don Lorenzo Milani hailed from Tuscany and was born into a very privileged family in Florence that bears the surname Comparetti, a well-known and prestigious surname in the Tuscan city. Milani's father was a university professor, his grandfather an archaeologist of repute and his great grandfather an internationally renowned philologist. Although he shared with Freire the experience of being raised in a predominantly Catholic country, Milani was certainly not religiously influenced by his parents. His mother declared herself an atheist in a 1970 interview and a footnote on the website, where this interview is reproduced, points out that she often referred to herself as agnostic. Milani's parents went through the motions of marrying through the Catholic Church but that was only because they were Jews and feared persecution from the Fascist government of the time. Surrounded by books, archaeological artefacts and leading intellectuals, as well as the wealth of the rentier classes, Milani was endowed with a cultural baggage which rendered his schooling, during the Fascist period, unappealing. Like Freire, he too had his mortifying moments as a child such as when he was pulled up by a woman for eating white bread in an alley inhabited by poor people, a social marker which must have made him aware of the social differences prevalent at the time, or when he would ask the family chauffer to drop him off at some distance from school, lest his school companions would see him being afforded such luxurious treatment in a city where there were only about fifteen private cars available, two of which were owned by Lorenzo's father (Fallaci, 1993, pp. 13, 14).

Milani had a very independent mind and he defied his family's aspirations for him by joining an art academy instead of a university. Nevertheless his family background gave him the confidence to speak his own mind, to be a livewire. It was probably through painting that he drew closer to the Catholic faith. He developed a profound interest in religious art and engaged in research on liturgy and colour so that he could capture the paintings' iconic significance. Much to his mother's chagrin, he eventually decided to receive holy confirmation and, years later, joined the seminary, eventually being ordained in 1947. Congratulated by Lorenzo's wet nurse, Carola Galastri, whose son was also ordained a priest, Lorenzo's mother – Alice Weiss – quipped 'bad milk' (Fallaci, 1993, p. 27), an indication of her feelings towards the priesthood and the Catholic faith in general, despite her profound love for her son which was reciprocated by Lorenzo throughout his short life.

Milani's priesthood continued to bring him in close contact with poor people and his feelings of solidarity with the oppressed (the poor and powerless) continued to be strengthened by his reading of the gospels and his clinging to an image of Christ whose option was for the poor – the meek who should inherit the earth. After a short spell at Montespertoli, he moved to the mainly working class and peasant inhabited San Donato di Calenzano where he led an evening 'popular school' (*scuola popolare*) for adults, which, he insisted, had to be devoid of all religious symbols to attract people of different political persuasions (Simeone, 1996, p. 99). Conversion was regarded by Milani as an act of grace and not something that can be taught (ibid.). He did not believe in the idea of a denominational school (*scuola confessionale*) which would have sharpened the social divisions in post-war Italy (ibid.). There was a strong secular feeling about his school which was not well received by the ecclesiastical authorities. His classes dealt with a range of subjects many of which related to class politics and oppression. Invited speakers were challenged by the course participants who were encouraged to prepare the topic beforehand, throughout the entire week, and engage in dialogue and a participatory approach. This and his own unorthodox approach to religion and pastoral work proved too much for sections of the San Donato community and certain priests based in the area. He was 'transferred', or 'exiled' if you will, to an obscure locality (Sant' Andrea a Barbiana), in the Mugello region, lacking even basic infrastructural amenities; the only road leading to the village came to an end a kilometre away. It was there that Milani developed his best-known educational project, a full time school for 'drop outs' of the public school system and developed an alternative radical pedagogy that has been a source of inspiration to teachers and social activists in Italy and elsewhere ever since. This was also the period when he wrote his controversial book (*Esperienze Pastorali* – Pastoral Experiences) and co-wrote, with his students, a series of letters including the famous *Lettera* and the letters in his defence of the right to conscientious objection to military conscription. He co-wrote many of these letters and taught, as well as administered the parish, while suffering from Hodgkin's disease which claimed his life at the age of 44.

UNDERLYING COMMON INFLUENCE: RADICAL CHRISTIANITY

It is clear from the biographical accounts that both educators were Christian- inspired. In Freire's case, the Christian precepts in his writings derive from a variety of sources notably the radical Catholic tradition in Brazil (De Kadt, 1970), the Christian personalism theory of Emanuel Mounier and the Brazilian, Christian de

Atiade and other figures connected with the Liberation Theology tradition by which he was influenced and on which he himself exerted an influence. Cardinal Paulo Evaristo Arns told the present author and a colleague (Carmel Borg) at the São Paulo Cathedral in April 1998 that Freire changed not only people's lives but also the church, with reference to the 1968 Episcopal Conference in Medellin (Mayo, 2004, p. 6). Freire very much belonged to the 'prophetic church' which he contrasts with the 'traditional' and 'modernizing' churches (Freire, 1985, p. 137). There is however another important influence on Freire, notably that of Marxism, comprising the work of Marx himself. One can argue therefore that there are two main strands in Freire's thinking, especially as expressed in his best-known work, *Pedagogy of the Oppressed* (Freire, 1993): Christianity and Marxism.

Milani is likewise eclectic in his writing and draws from various sources but the underlying source in his work is that of Christianity with the main impetus deriving from the Gospels. While Marxist writers must have appealed to Milani and he certainly used Gramsci's *Letters from Prison* as one of the reading texts at the School of Barbiana, there is no evidence of Marxist thinking serving as an important underlying current in his writings. The *Lettera*, written under his direction, is devoid of the sort of theoretical references one finds in, for instance, *Pedagogy of the Oppressed*. It is less erudite in this regard but no less powerful in the force of its argument. Milani's attitude towards socialism is somewhat ambivalent. He criticized the Italian Communist Party (PCI) and the Catholic Church for vying with each other and, consequently, selling young working class people short in the various Italian localities with which he was familiar. In his view, they placed more emphasis on entertainment, such as carnival balls (Milani, 2004), than on education, with a view to swelling membership in the PCI's case or winning over souls in the case of the Catholic Church. Milani was not averse to socialism as an ideology per se, despite his occasional reference to the excesses of the so-called socialismo reale (actually existing socialism) in the Soviet Union and the rest of the Eastern Bloc (Freire was equally critical of such excesses). In fact, Milani is on record as saying that democracy and socialism are 'the two noblest political systems mankind has yet been given' (Milani, 1988a, p. 25) and he considered socialism 'the highest attempt of humankind to give, already on this earth, justice and equality to the poor' (ibid., p. 26).

Freire, for his part, became a founding member of the socialist oriented PT in Brazil and even served as education secretary in São Paulo on behalf of the PT. Milani and his pupils, writing in the *Lettera*, express an almost cynical attitude towards parties in Italy. They do not differentiate between the dominant parties in Italian political life, the 'partiti dei laureati' (graduates' political parties), which allow representatives of the dominant social classes to legislate on behalf of the poor. 'But first we have to get into Parliament. Whites will never make the laws needed by the blacks' (School of Barbiana, 1969, p. 53). The assumption here is that even those parties that ostensibly represent the interests of the working class, the socialist and communist parties, are the preserve of the most influential families and the ruling class in Italian society. Of course, the thinking on this subject is conditioned by the particular situation obtaining in the Italian context, a situation in which members of the same family (e.g. the influential Berlinguer-Segni-Cossiga family from Sassari) can occupy leadership positions on different sides of the national political spectrum. They also mention the mechanism whereby working class and peasant class people who make it through the system, against the odds, and enter parliament are often 'embourgeoised' in the process. Milani's dreamt not of the 'liberation' of people from farming but of a liberated farmer content with living a sober life.

These context-conditioned differences notwithstanding, there is something that strongly connects Milani's ideas concerning society and education to those espoused by Freire, namely an underlying option for the oppressed and a commitment to an education for social justice. Theirs was a vision steeped in modernity and its concomitant notion of an emancipatory education. They both believed in a world not as it is now but as it can and should be.

EDUCATION FOR SOCIAL JUSTICE

Paulo Freire will be always identified by educators for his pedagogy of the oppressed. Education, for Freire, is not neutral and involves educating for either domestication or liberation. It involves taking sides. The same applies to Milani who, in his Letter to the Military Chaplains, states forcefully:

> If you persist in claiming the right to divide the world into Italians and foreigners, then I must say to you that, in your view of things, I have no Fatherland. I would then want the right to divide the world into disinherited and oppressed on one side, and privileged and oppressors on the other. One group is my Fatherland; to me the others are foreigners. (1988a, p. 19)

In the words of one of his former students, Edoardo Martinelli (one of the eight authors of the *Lettera*), 'There was obviously nothing really neutral about Don Milani. He believed in a committed educator, one who takes sides: "Better a fascist than indifferent!"' (Martinelli, in Borg and Mayo, 2007, p. 113). Echoing Amilcar Cabral, Paulo Freire had argued that the revolutionary activist, and by implication the revolutionary educator, would have to commit 'class suicide', that is renounce his or her former state of privilege to work on the side of and *with*, not *for*, the oppressed. To what extent this is possible is quite arguable given the difficulties involved in 'jumping out of one's skin'. It is more likely that one has to engage critically and tenaciously with one's contradictory consciousness in these circumstances (Mayo, 1999).

Don Lorenzo Milani came close to the idea of a person committing class suicide or, to use Freire's more Christian metaphor, experiencing his Easter. He denounced his own education which reflected his country's imperialistic ambitions:

> They presented the Empire to us as a glory for the Fatherland! I was thirteen at the time; it seems as if it were today. I jumped with joy for the Empire. Our teachers neglected to tell us that the Ethiopians were superior to us. We were going to burn down their huts with their women and children inside, while they had done nothing to us.
>
> That was a cowardly school which – wittingly or unwittingly, I cannot say – prepared for us the horrors to follow in three years' time. It prepared millions of obedient soldiers, obedient to the orders of Mussolini. To be more precise, obedient to the orders of Hitler. Fifty million people died. (Milani, 1988b, p. 65)

Denouncing this type of chauvinistic education at the time was no difficult task given that the period of schooling referred to occurred during the Fascist period, much vilified in the post-war years. Milani however went a step further and held the social class to which he belonged responsible for the horrors of the imperialistic wars described earlier (Milani, 1991, p. 42; Milani, 1988b, p. 62; Scuola di Barbiana, 1996, p. 74). Despite being a Jew, an ethnic marker which made one ever so liable to persecution by the Fascists at the behest of Hitler, he was also a member of that same bourgeoisie that was responsible for the terrible turn of events in Italian politics (the turn to fascism) to safeguard its privileges and avert its crisis of hegemony. Conscious of the fact that resources were limited and highly suspicious of the emerging consumerism at the time, he chose a life of sobriety, austerity and poverty, a practical renunciation of the life to which he was born and in which he was bred. Once again, Edoardo Martinelli states: 'He did live his sober life not as a form of penance, abstinence or simply Christian living but as a way of embracing the values and pleasures that can be satisfied and learnt only through poverty.' And yet the earlier reference to the 'partiti dei laureati' (graduates' political parties) would suggest that Milani and the Barbiana students would be among the first to recognize the limits of class suicide. They seem to doubt whether people from wealthy families can, despite their allegiances and ethical commitment to the subaltern classes, 'jump out of their skin' and break away from their 'habitus'.

These contradictions notwithstanding, both Freire and Milani would agree on regarding educating as a political act. Both see traditional educational institutions as bourgeois institutions and conventional teaching, marked by what Freire would call 'banking education', as an activity which serves to support the status quo in a society marked by 'cultural invasion' and what Pierre Bourdieu would regard as the 'cultural arbitrary' of the dominant sectors of society. Repetition and ultimately exclusion was the case with the compulsory schooling of students from the subaltern social strata in Italy during Milani's time. This was the experience of Gianni from whose point of view the *Lettera* is written. It is written in a tone of anger that results from the recognition of the 'symbolic violence' meted out by a public school system that serves to reproduce class hierarchies. What is ostensibly a 'fair' public education system, intended to provide opportunities for all citizens, according to the terms of the constitution, is in effect a subtle way of reproducing the class system on the basis of a contestable notion of 'meritocracy':

> The poor man [Gianni's father] – if he knew what was going on I would pick up his weapon and be a Partisan again. There are teachers who coach for money in their free time. So, instead of removing the obstacles they work to deepen the differences among students. (School of Barbiana, 1969, p. 35)

The schooling system, as countless educational sociologists have underlined over the years, backed by endless research, favours the 'cultural capital' of the middle class. In contrast to the figure of Gianni, in the *Lettera*, we find that of Pierino, the 'doctor's son (ibid., p. 25), who enters school with a significant head-start, who finds the scholastic experience a natural extension to the culture of the home, who moves easily through the various grades and who 'at nine, finds himself in the class for ten to eleven years olds' (ibid., p. 29). Unlike Gianni, whose father 'went to work at age twelve and did not finish the fourth year level of schooling' (ibid., p. 34), Pierino can afford to have less formal schooling since he can avail himself of the materially rewarding 'cultural capital' derived from home and its surrounding milieu (ibid., p. 48). This is the reason why Milani helped develop a school 'a tempo pieno' (full time) at Barbiana, including weekends. Like Bourdieu and Passeron (1990), the authors of the *Lettera* state:

> You say that little Pierino, daddy's boy, can write well. But, of course, he speaks as you do. He is part of the firm. (ibid, p. 12)
>
> He too, is already branded, but with the mark of the chosen race. (ibid., p. 25)

While Freire must have felt the same way about formal schooling, he was also aware of the fact that, in his native Brazil, very few pupils had access to public education where the 'drop out' rate after 1 or 2 years was alarming.

While Freire has stated time and time again that we should not romanticize education and accord it powers it does not have, he still believed in agency and in the potential for education to serve a democratic and liberating purpose. Unlike radical contemporaries such as Illich, he saw schools as sites of contestation and it is for this reason that, when he was in his late 60s, he and his team took on the onerous task of reforming the public school sector in São Paulo with a view to turning public schools into places that appeal and belong to the traditionally socially marginalized classes rather than places that are perceived as being antagonistic towards these same classes. The school was intended to constitute a key institution in the development of a truly democratic and popular 'public sphere', the term being used in Habermas' sense. He introduced the notion of a 'popular public' school which incorporated some of the principles associated with the type of popular education with which he is associated. This was a community school not unlike that developed by Milani and his students from Barbiana and the surrounding areas. Freire and Milani seem to be in agreement on one very important issue namely that a liberating and democratic education belongs to not the world of 'having' but the world of 'being'. They also concur that there is no method and there are no techniques involved in providing this alternative type of education. Freire reiterated this point time and time again, rejecting what has come to be regarded as the 'fetish of method' (see Allman, 1996; Aronowitz, 1993; Macedo, 1994; Macedo in Freire and Macedo, 1995). Milani responded, when asked the irritating question regarding what was the success of his approach at the adult education classes in San Donato, with the following statement, written in his controversial *Esperienze Pastorali*:

> They ask the wrong question. They should be preoccupied not with what *one has to do to teach* but with *how one should be* in order to teach. (My translation from Milani, 1996, p. 80)

In Milani's view, teaching and learning involved 'being' rather than 'how to do'. 'Being' (Essere) entailed having clear ideas about social and political issues (ibid.), the mark of those who educate for a critical citizenship. Both are in agreement that, to use Freire's words, experiments cannot be transplanted but must be reinvented. Milani was adamant that the Barbiana experience could not be reproduced elsewhere. It was an experience related to place and context. Freire always spoke about the need to reinvent the political pedagogical approach he promoted and not try to apply it in cargo-cult style. In short, the Barbiana and Freirean experiments served as sources of inspiration and as means to stimulate the imagination of those who tend to educate for a world not as it is now but as it should and can be – stimulate and inspire, yes but not transplant.

Furthermore, both related *education* to *life*, in this respect echoing Dewey with his emphasis on education and experience (Dewey, 1938). They argued for an education that had to be culturally relevant and not culturally alienating as was the hallmark of the traditional school that bored the life out of working class children. In the words of Edoardo Martinelli:

> The schooling of that period – I would dare say that the same could well apply to contemporary schooling – was based on the strict transmission of ministerial programs. These programs were carried out 'to the letter' with the teacher being allowed little autonomy. Everything was planned to the extent that we students (there were several of us around, with different backgrounds) could anticipate the events, the questions and the title of the subjects to be tackled. We hardly came across anything that was unexpected and there were no situations that led to the adoption of pedagogical strategies that automatically connected with our interests, motivations and environments. The agenda was the same year in year out. I recall that I struggled to cope at school and I hated almost every subject.
>
> I could not perceive, at the time, the connection between learning and life. When I arrived at Barbiana, everything was different. The point of reference for the group's learning was life itself and this entailed an active research process. The learning setting itself was dynamic. (Martinelli, in Borg and Mayo, 2007, p. 110)

Foreign language teaching and acquisition constitutes one example of the manner in which Milani insisted on relating learning to life. He sent his pupils abroad to work in various cities to earn enough for their upkeep while they resided there. This was intended for them not simply to cross borders and broaden their horizons but also to learn foreign languages as spoken by the native speakers themselves. This approach stood in marked contrast to the artificial way by which foreign languages were taught and examined in the Italian public school system. Working and peasant class students often failed tests, the contents of which had no bearing on the kind of life lived within and outside the student's own region. As the authors of the *Lettera* say, the French learnt by Pierino, which enabled him to pass the state exam, would not allow him to find the way to the toilet in France (Scuola di Barbiana, 1996, p. 21).

In keeping with the Marxist tradition, Freire regards one's material surroundings as the basis for the development of one's consciousness. In the words of Marx and Engels: 'Consciousness is, therefore, from the beginning a social product, and remains so as long as men [*sic*]) exist at all' (Marx and Engels, 1970, p. 51). Freire's process of education based on 'cultural action' is concerned with the relationship between knowledge and one's material existence. For Freire, the starting point is always that of human beings 'in the "here and now"', that is the human beings' current situation 'from which they emerge, and in which they intervene' (Freire, 1993, p. 85). It is for this reason that, in his adult education work, members of the cultural circles researched the community, analysing its issues and codifying them. It is also for this reason that teachers from the schools that elected to join his 'popular public' schools project in São Paulo researched the community to derive generative themes. These generative themes are conceived of, in the words of O'Cadiz et al., as 'the building blocks for the construction of a locally relevant curriculum' (O'Cadiz et al., 1998, p. 85). Likewise Milani used events or developments within the community that captured the students' imagination and used them as motivating factors for lessons in a variety of areas. Martinelli discloses that, when he entered the classroom at Barbiana, he saw Don Milani and the rest of the class analyse skeletons in what was an anatomy lesson.

> The immediate motive, the key point of departure for his pedagogical activity, was provided by the fact that the floor of the society, which stood adjacent to the church, caved in. Bones were discovered as a result. The more profound and long term motive, as he explained in the letter to the Judges, with reference to his pedagogical practice, was to avail himself of this particular event to capture the pupils' interest and thus gradually lead them, once they had become so motivated, to tackle the core areas of the disciplines. A few bones were sufficient to enable one to learn how to use vocabulary and texts dealing with anatomy and physiology. These subjects were non-existent in the middle schools of the period. This is how we learnt to read, write and count. (Martinelli, in Borg and Mayo, 2007, p. 110)

The operative word here is 'lead' for the 'here and now' constituted only the starting point of the lesson and was meant to lead to the disciplines. The same applies to Freire for whom the learner's concrete situation is the point of departure for their knowledge of the world (Freire, 1994, p. 85). Once again, it is only the starting point, however, and not the be all and end all of the pedagogical encounter (see Freire, 1994, p. 84). In Dewey's words: 'But finding the material for learning within experience is only the first step. The next step is the progressive development of what is already experienced into a fuller and richer and also more organized form, a form that gradually approximates that in which subject-matter is presented to the skilled mature person' (Dewey, 1938, pp. 73–4).

In remaining there and not moving beyond (through co-investigation of the object of inquiry), and therefore not engaging in *praxis* (obtaining a critical distance from one's world of action to reflect on it for transformative action), one would be engaging in 'the romanticization (or "mythification") of the vernacular' (ibid.). O'Cadiz et al. (1998) also point out, in their analysis of the school reforms in São Paulo carried out by the Freire-led Education Secretariat, that the generative themes, researched by teachers and other community members, provide only an 'initial' step in engaging students and teachers in a critical reading of their world (p. 87).

From Freire's perspective, the best way to engage the learner's framework of relevance is to allow space for the learners themselves to engage critically with the issues, to bring their own insights, culture and different aspects of their multiple subjectivities to bear on the learning process. This is the antithesis of 'banking education' and the ministerial programmes to which Martinelli refers. It is for this reason that Freire underlines the importance of 'authentic dialogue' as the key to a truly liberating education, one through which the dialectical relationship of opposites between dominating teacher and submissive student, and therefore between oppressor and oppressed, is transformed. Although stressing that both competent teacher and student are never on an equal footing and that one must distinguish between having authority (bestowed on the teacher by the student who recognizes the teacher's competence in the area and as a pedagogue and has faith in the teacher) and being authoritarian, Freire recognizes possibilities for critical consciousness in a learning setting where the learners are encouraged to participate through dialogue. Once again, it is a situation where the educators are disposed, through humility and love, to relearn that which they think they already know through interaction with the learners. The latter have the potential, as a result of their own studies, preparation and different social locations (these can result in different perspectives on the matter at issue) to re-educate the educator, in the sense employed by Marx in the 'Third Thesis on Feuerbach', as well as fellow learners in a process of development of 'group knowledge' (Mannheim, 1936, p. 29). Once again, we have teacher–student and students–teachers who regard knowledge as not static but dynamic, an object of co-investigation.

This should serve to provide students with the impetus to learn and 'become more', that is, to develop greater coherence, as Freire wrote in his later work (Freire, 1997), using a less essentialist phrase than his earlier one of persons 'becoming more fully human' (Freire, 1993). This process of learning serves as an antidote to the kind of boring and alienating education associated with the 'banking' type of education, the kind of education which led the Giannis or Giannas to be pushed out of the public schools in Italy after they failed their summative exam. Milani too believed in dialogue and the *conferenza del venerdi* (the Friday conference) at San Donato provided an excellent example of this approach. Workers and peasants prepared the material beforehand to avoid being ostensibly 'passive' listeners (as Freire and others have shown one is never really a passive listener since one derives different meanings from what is being presented without necessarily giving voice to this meaning). They were encouraged to engage the speaker. Milani often pulled up the speaker for a lack of adequate preparation and communication, as is evident from a letter to a certain Dott. Gozzini (Milani, 1970, p. 37).

Milani formalized the students–teachers role at Barbiana for logistical as well as pedagogical reasons. He introduced peer tutoring/teaching realizing that pupils often learn better from their own peers with whom they share the same social class and broader cultural background and therefore language. In a school which placed the emphasis on caring, with the motto 'I Care' written on one of the school walls in English (Milani, 1991, p. 34; Milani, 1988b, p. 56), the students engaged in a pedagogical experience in which they were both teachers and learners. Milani himself tutored the first group of students. As students increased in number – there were around 40 students in one particular summer – he adopted peer tutoring as a key pedagogical tool. The older students, while learning from

Milani and other students of more or less the same age, also taught the younger ones.

> There was just one copy of each book. The boys would pile up around it. It was hard to notice that one of them was a bit older and was teaching. The oldest of these teachers was sixteen. The youngest was twelve, and filled me with admiration. I made up my mind from the start that I, too, was going to teach. (School of Barbiana, 1969, p. 8)

Older students could spend a whole morning teaching their younger counterparts.

> The next year I was a teacher, that is, three half-days a week. I taught Geography, Mathematics and French to the first intermediate year. (Ibid., p. 9)

Here was a 'caring' educational relationship based on learning not for one to 'have' (possessive knowledge and individualism) but to 'be' and to 'be' for others, to adopt Eric Fromm's distinction. It must have served as a tremendous source of motivation for the students, once degraded and therefore demoralized by the public schools, to now be 'elevated' to the status of and esteemed as teachers. It is hardly surprising that they would exclaim, in the *Lettera*, with reference to the long periods of time spent at school and its extended learning setting, 'School will always be better than cow shit' (School of Barbiana, 1969, p. 9; Scuola di Barbiana, 1996, p. 13). This source of motivation made them serve as educators as well as learners (gladly will they teach and gladly will they learn, as Chaucer wrote about the Clerk in the *Canterbury Tales*) in the same way that cultural circle members, as presented by Freire, served this dual role through a process of authentic dialogue: students–teachers and teacher–student.

An authentic dialogical approach necessitates the sharpening of listening skills. To engage in dialogue, educators must stop suffering from 'narration sickness' (Freire, 1993, p. 71) and become 'listeners'. One would find instructive Freire's illuminating reflection on the notion of 'listening' as opposed to hearing in *Pedagogy of Freedom* (Freire, 1998b, p. 107).

Writing on the San Donato experience, in *Esperienze Pastorali*, Lorenzo Milani states that he derived many insights and ideas from the peasants themselves:

> I owe everything that I know to the young workers and peasants with whom I carried out schooling. It is I who have learnt from them that which they believe to be learning from me. I have only taught them to express themselves while they have taught me to live. It is they who have led me to think those thoughts that are expressed in this book. I have never found them in schoolbooks. I learnt them as I was writing them and I wrote them because they [*the workers and peasants*] placed them in my heart. (My translation from Milani, 1996, p. 76)

Of course, like Freire, Milani also believed in a directive form of education, the alternative to which would have been *laissez-faire* pedagogy, denounced by Freire. Allowing his students to indulge in *laissez-faire* pedagogy would have been a case of utter irresponsibility on Milani's part, given the age of the students and Barbiana and Milani's concern for their future in a society where knowledge is power. Having said this, he did believe in the students' autonomy as learners. Suffice to mention that when he left San Donato and took up residence in Barbiana, the Friday conference continued to be carried out by the youths of San Donato themselves and he assisted them from afar by establishing contact with potential speakers, as indicated in one of his letters to Elena Brambilla, dated 20 June 1961 (Milani, 1970, pp. 147–8). He also had faith in the Barbiana boys' ability to learn on their own by working and living abroad, for a period of time, in places located not only in Europe but also in North Africa.

The emphasis on dialogue and learning from each other both in Freire's cultural circles and in the learning settings which Milani helped create in tandem with community members (at San Donato) and his students (at Barbiana) underlines an important aspect of an education intended to serve as an antidote to that which predominates in a capitalist world. Both Milani and Freire underlined the *collective* dimensions of knowledge. This approach remains relevant in an age when we are bombarded with such phrases as 'self-directed learning', 'individualized modules' and so on. The knowledge promoted by Freire in the dialogical circle was 'group knowledge'. Freire argued that one engages in the task of becoming more fully human not on one's own but in solidarity with others (Freire, 1993, pp. 85–6). Freire argues, in this context, that, in adopting an individualistic approach to being human, one would be denying others the chance of attaining the same state (i.e. being authentically human). This individualistic endeavour would entail a dehumanizing process of 'having more' (ibid.).

Like the cultural circle, the School of Barbiana provided a learning space that affirmed the collective dimensions of learning in contrast to the dominant compulsory school that promoted a notion of citizenship predicated on the ideology of competitive individualism so endemic to capitalist social relations. The 'I Care' motto points to this. The programme at Barbiana was based on a politics of solidarity and caring. Not only did pupils care but we have seen how their caring also took the form of a collective pedagogical experience in which they were both teachers and learners. Furthermore, the chronicles of the time served as an important source of learning at Barbiana. The afternoon lesson at Barbiana centred on the facts of the day as reported by the local newspaper. This lesson combined knowledge of current affairs with the teaching of such skills as critical analysis and *critical literacy*, in Paulo Freire's sense of the term. This represents an attempt to read the world through a critical engagement with this world's construction via the media:

> I also knew well the history of my own time. That means the daily newspaper, which we always read at Barbiana, aloud, from top to bottom. (School of Barbiana, 1969, p. 17)

Current events and controversies were followed carefully, articles were engaged with collectively, their underlying ideological positions were identified and unveiled, as Freire would put it, and this exercise in critical literacy often provoked *collective* responses by the students working in tandem with their mentor. Echoing a point made by Paul V. Taylor in a book on Freire (Taylor, 1993), the Barbiana pupils not only read but also wrote the world and, I would add, they did so *collectively* and *critically*.

Perhaps the major contribution to an education with a collective dimension is provided by the following aspect of the teaching/learning process at Barbiana. In keeping with the 'I Care' motto at the school, the class did not proceed to the next stage in the learning process until each and every pupil mastered the last one. Rather than fail pupils, the school gave priority to the child who fell backward. As argued elsewhere (Borg and Mayo, 2006, p. 143), 'unlike elitist educational systems which stream and track students according to perceived "ability", creating in the process the context for high expectations for largely privileged students (the Pierinos/as) and lower expectations (a "cooling out" process) and less resources for mostly working class, disabled and non-white students', the Barbiana School accorded pride of place to those who did not keep abreast. The Barbiana School is instructive regarding 'how educational institutions, especially those run by the Church, can consciously choose to educate the least privileged as part of a genuine option for the poor' (Borg and Mayo, 2006, p. 143):

> But there a boy who had no background, who was slow or lazy [*sic*], was made to feel like the favourite. He would be treated the way you teachers treat the best student in the class. It seemed as if the school was meant just for him. Until he could be made to understand, the others would not continue. (Ibid., p. 8)

The Barbiana School favoured an education system that, involving a collective group effort, does not give up easily on the child:

> You would wake up at night thinking about him and would try to invent new ways to teach him – ways that would fit his needs. You would go to fetch him from home if he did not show up for class. (Ibid., p. 47)

This standpoint provided elements that add credibility and forcefulness to the arguments developed throughout the *Lettera*. Certainly teachers play an important role in providing a social justice education predicated on an option for the poor and less privileged members of society. They are not the only important players in this process but nevertheless their role remains crucial. This explains why people who promote a critical approach to education accord a strong sense of agency to socially conscious educators acting as transformative cultural workers (Giroux, 1988) 'in and against' a bourgeois-oriented and therefore biased school system. Teachers play a crucial role within Freire's conception of schools as sites of contestation, although Freire emphasizes the importance of teachers having one foot 'tactically' inside and another foot 'strategically' outside the educational system. In the latter case they would be rooted within progressive social movements, the kind of movements Paulo Freire sought to involve, in his educational reforms in São Paulo when he served as education secretary.

And it is in the portrayal of teachers that I note an important difference between Freire and Milani or rather, in the latter case, the boys who wrote the *Lettera* under Milani's direction. Despite his portrayal, in a rather mechanistic fashion, of what the teacher does under conditions of 'Banking Education', Freire presents teachers in a very positive light in his written works, especially those penned in the latter stages of his life. He had struggled hard, as education secretary, to improve the conditions of teachers:

> It is urgent that we drum up more support in this country for public schools that are popular, effective, democratic, and happy and whose teachers are well paid, well trained and in constant development. Never again should teachers' salaries be astronomically lower than those of the presidents and directors of government corporations, as they are today . . . It is not acceptable on the eve of the new millennium that we continue to experience the alarming quantitative and qualitative deficits that currently exist in our education. We cannot enter the new millennium with thousands of so-called lay teachers, even in the poor areas of the country, sometimes making less than the minimum wage. They are heroic people, giving, loving, intelligent people, but people treated with contempt by national oligarchies. (Freire, 1998a, p. 35)

Furthermore, Freire expressed his concern that the teacher's competence was being undermined through the imposition by a 'half a dozen self-proclaimed specialists' of content-oriented 'packages' and manuals or guides that describe how to use these packages (Freire, 1998c, p. 67). Freire regards such an imposition of teacher-proof material as indicative of an authoritarian disregard for 'the critical capacity of teachers, their knowledge or their practice' (ibid.) and an authoritarian attempt 'to instill in teachers a fear of freedom' (Freire, 1998a, p. 9). In contrast, Freire not only advocated but helped develop policies, with his secretariat's team and other stakeholders in education, which enabled teachers to work collaboratively across disciplines to create an interdisciplinary curriculum (O'Cadiz et al., 1998, p. 93). In short, teachers were conceived of as people with the ability to reflect on and engage critically with issues and not as technicians executing decisions communicated to them from afar.

One comes across a different portrayal of teachers in the *Lettera*. These are persons who flunk students, assess them on skills they did not enable the students to acquire (the authors point to the teacher's inane assertion that 'writers are born and not made', to which they retort: 'Meanwhile you receive a salary as a teacher of Italian' – School of Barbiana, 1969, p. 74) and exacerbate the social divisions between the Giannis and the Pierinos by providing extra tuition to the latter against payment (School of Barbiana, 1969, p. 35). With respect to the last point, they write:

> In the morning – during regular school hours – we pay them to give the same schooling to all. Later on in the day they get money from richer people to school their young gentlemen differently. Then, in June, at our expense, they preside at the trial and judge the differences. (Ibid., p. 35)

LESSONS FROM FREIRE, MILANI AND THE SAN DONATO/BARBIANA EXPERIENCES

Did the School of Barbiana give up on teachers in the public school system? On the contrary, the School of Barbiana experience provides an alternative form of schooling from which teachers in the public school system can learn. Much depends on the attitude that the teachers develop, as indicated by Milani when stating that it is more a question of how one must be, rather than what one must do, to be able to teach in a manner that is meaningful to one's students. Teachers can provide such an alternative education by: calling for and engaging in a 'doposcuola' (after school) programme which is provided to everyone and not just those who can pay for it; by encouraging peer tutoring; by enabling students to learn collectively and 'to be' not just for themselves but also and mainly for others; by relating education to life; by starting with the 'here and now' and moving beyond to higher order thinking; by engaging *with* learners in a critical reading of the world (*praxis*) as manifest in its day to day reality but also through its construction via the media; by being disposed to learn and relearn what one thinks one already knows from the pupils themselves who have a lot to offer in terms of insights derived from their different cultural backgrounds and specific abilities; by calling for an inclusive curriculum that is relevant to the different pupils in the classroom and a school which does not fail students and push them out but ensures that the constitutional right of everyone to enjoy a number of years of public schooling (that does not involve repetition) is respected and safeguarded.

The fact that a number of pupils from the Barbiana experience ended up as teachers indicates that they had faith in the emergence of a type of teacher who was different from the one portrayed in a negative light in the *Lettera*. They had faith in a teacher concerned with social justice issues and who sees her or his mission in life as one intended to improve the life chances and experiences of those who have traditionally suffered in a socially differentiated system. This is the type of teacher that Freire sought to inspire, a teacher whose attitude and efforts are motivated by feelings of love, humility and social solidarity. And the verb 'calling for' in the list of qualities just provided, a list serving as a brief concluding synthesis of the ideas of Freire, Milani and the Schools of San Donato and Barbiana, indicates that many of the challenges cannot be faced by teachers on their own. As Freire would argue, they can only be faced by teachers within a movement or alliance of movements calling for reforms in the state school system, reforms that would thus help revitalize an important sector of the public sphere.

CHAPTER 10

Julius Nyerere's Thinking on Education

Julius Nyerere has had many detractors and continues to do so today, 13 years following his death. Freire was however not one of them as I shall show later on in this chapter. He is, however, one of Africa's best-known and most revered postcolonial figures. A devout Catholic, son of a village chief in Butiama (northern Tanzania) and a former school teacher in a Catholic school, Julius Kambarage Nyerere (1922–99) had an eventful life which saw him lead Tanganyika to independence in 1961, become its president and eventually become the first president of Tanzania following the unification of Tanganyika and Zanzibar in 1964. There seems to have been some kind of mutual admiration between Nyerere and Freire and the latter was invited to Tanzania to oversee the literacy programme which had brought the country fame worldwide especially in the eyes of UNESCO.

Constantly projecting the image of someone who can lead by example, 'Mwalimu' ('teacher' in Kiswahili), as Nyerere was called, remained at the helm of Tanzanian politics even following his retirement as president. He was, until 1990, Head of *Chama Cha Mapinduzi* (party of revolution), the party which grew out of the 1977 merger between TANU (Tanganyikan National Union) and *Afro-Shirazi*, Zanzibar's ruling party. Tanzania eventually witnessed the transition, under Nyerere's successor as president, Ali Hassan Mwinyi, from a one party to a multiparty state. Many would regard Nyerere's project of socialism for the East African country to have failed in material terms, as did capitalist projects in other African countries, for that matter: 'A bunch of countries [*in Africa*] were in economic shambles at the end of the 70s. They are not socialists', Nyerere reminds us in a transcribed 1996 interview with an American correspondent (Nyerere, 1996). There are those who openly expressed their reservations concerning the viability of his socialist project for Tanzania. His policies have been praised in certain quarters and decried in others, as one can gather from the different and contrasting appraisals of his work, appearing in the international press, following his death towards the end of 1999. Many are those, however, who recognize Nyerere's stature as a statesman and opinion leader. The country stood out, in comparison with other African countries, for its peaceful transition of power and for its lack of ethnic strife. He states: 'Complete integration of the separate racial systems was introduced very soon after independence, and discrimination on the grounds of religion was brought to an end' (Nyerere, 1968, p. 270).

At the time of his death, Mwalimu Nyerere had been playing a prominent role in the quest for a solution to the terrible tribal power conflicts in the Great Lakes region of East Africa (he acted as chief mediator in Burundi [Smith, 1999, p. 9] to avoid a communal catastrophe reminiscent of nearby Rwanda). He was deeply involved in development politics, having chaired the South Commission and more recently the Intergovernmental South Centre (Smith, 1999, p. 9) in Geneva.

There are those who feel that his vision of Pan-Africanism remains unparalleled among African leaders. During his presidency, Tanzania provided support and shelter for a host of African freedom fighters, including ANC (African National Congress) activists and others combating Portuguese colonialism. Furthermore, Nyerere was one of the founding figures of the Non-Aligned Movement. He was also instrumental in the overthrow of Idi Amin in Uganda.

He had his problems on the international scene. There were problems with Western countries which had led to foreign aid cutbacks. These consisted of: conflicts with the United Kingdom, following the latter's recognition of the unilateral Declaration of Independence by white settlers in Rhodesia; conflicts with West Germany following Tanzania's recognition of the DDR (German Democratic Republic); conflicts with the United States following accusations by Tanzania of CIA involvement in the East African country (Unsicker, 1986, p. 232). Nyerere's particular brand of socialism appeared to have incurred the wrath of several communists, especially those from the Eastern Bloc (Okoh, 1980, p. 52). Capitalism was obnoxious to Nyerere who is on record as having said, at one time, that he differed from Western socialists precisely on the grounds that they glorify capitalism as a mode of production that begets socialism (ibid.).

His writings on development, socialism, literature (he translated Shakespeare's *Julius Caesar* [*Juliasi Kaizari*] and the *Merchant of Venice* [*Mabepari wa Venisi*] into Kiswahili), education, African liberation, intellectuals, non-alignment and a host of other subjects constitute an often cited corpus of postcolonial writing to come out of Africa.

One area in which Julius Nyerere is often cited is that of *Education* (see Kassam, 1994; Samoff, 1990; Smith, 1999) and this is hardly surprising given the importance he attached to this domain of social policy and practice in his writings and work as leader of Tanzania.

Nyerere's overarching political concept was that of *Ujamaa* (familyhood) which represents an attempt by a third world leader to apply socialism to the specific needs of an African community. It rests on three basic tenets, expressed in his famous tract on education 'Education for Self-Reliance': 'equality and respect for human dignity; sharing of the resources which are produced by our efforts; work by everyone and exploitation by none' (Nyerere, 1968, p. 272). TANU established these basic ideals in the national ethic as well as in the Arusha Declaration (Nyerere, 1968, pp. 231–50), the latter being the declaration of policy which the country had to follow. Recently, Nyerere expounded on these socialist values which he considered still pertinent in an age in which we are swamped by neoliberalism and its concomitant ideology of the marketplace. According to the transcript of the 1996 interview, he stated:

> And those values are values of justice, a respect for human beings, a development which is people-centered, development where you care about people . . . you can say leave the development of a country to something called the market which has no heart at all since capitalism is completely ruthless . . . who is going to help the poor? . . . and the majority of the people in our countries are poor. Who is going to stand for them? Not the market. So I'm not regretting that I tried to build a country based on those principles. You will have to—whether you call them socialism or not – do you realize that what made – what gave capitalism a human face was the kind of values I was trying to sell in my country. (Nyerere, 1996)

The Nigerian scholar J. D. Okoh states that the first principle in the Arusha Declaration, that of respect for human dignity, was stressed in view of the fact that 'several decades of colonization had created in the African a deep-seated "inferiority complex", coupled with a crisis of identity' (Okoh, 1980, p. 54). Okoh refers to Nyerere's statement that it was once a compliment rather than an insult to refer to a person harbouring a European mentality as a 'Black European', a statement which is reminiscent of Frantz Fanon's (1952) 'Black Skin, White Masks'. This is typical of the colonial ideology which often involves, in Freire's terms, an internalization of the image of the oppressor (Freire, 1970, p. 32). Drawing from my experience as a native of a country (Malta) with a long history of direct colonization, I would submit that this often takes the form of pathetically *aping* the demeanour and other attributes (including spoken language) of the colonizer.

The second principle in the Arusha Declaration, stressing the need to share resources, suggests the idea of communitarianism that is at the heart of Ujamaa. Nyerere regarded this as an attempt to recuperate what he regarded to be the traditional African experience which was destroyed by the colonial powers through their notorious policy of 'divide and rule'. Okoh quotes him as having placed emphasis on recuperating a mindset that gives one the security deriving from one's sense of belonging to a 'widely extended family' (Okoh, 1980, p. 52), even though the same author is quick to point out that many African scholars criticized Nyerere for romanticizing pre-colonial African society. This notion of familyhood led many to regard his political credo as 'Christian socialism'.

His concept of grassroots democracy revolved around Ujamaa or, more appropriately, in this case, *Ujamaa Vijijni* (village familyhood), which entailed a process of participatory democracy. Writing in *Freedom and Development*, a policy booklet published in 1968, Nyerere says:

> [E]veryone must be allowed to speak freely, and everyone must be listened to. It does not matter how unpopular a man's ideas, or how mistaken the majority think him. It does not make any difference whether he is liked or disliked for his personal qualities. Every Tanzanian, every member of a community, every member of a District Council, every Member of Parliament, and so on, must have the freedom to speak without fear of intimidation – either inside or outside the meeting place [*sic*]' (1974, pp. 30, 31)

In a very important evaluative document, published 10 years after the Arusha Declaration, Nyerere took political leaders to task for not listening to the people. He states: 'They find it much easier to

TELL people what to do. Meetings are often monologues, without much, if any, time being devoted to discussion; and even then the speech is usually an exhortation to work hard rather than an explanation to do things better' (Nyerere, 1977, p. 29). Moreover, in *Freedom and Development*, Nyerere states that people should not be forced into joining the 'Ujamaa Vijijni' and stresses that the concept is based on the post-Arusha Declaration understanding that what Tanzania needs 'to develop is people, not things, and that people can only develop themselves' (Nyerere, 1974, p. 36).

The idea of a participatory communal being was in marked reaction to the very limited and elitist colonial education in place in Tanganyika and Zanzibar at the time of independence. In 'Education for Self-Reliance', Nyerere argues that colonial education 'was based on the assumptions of a colonialist and capitalist society. It emphasised and encouraged the individualistic instincts of mankind, instead of his co-operative instincts [*sic*]. It led to the possession of individual material wealth being the criterion of social merit and worth' (Nyerere, 1968, p. 269). The colonial educational provision was characterized by what Paulo Freire (1970, p. 151) would call 'cultural invasion', a process which undermined traditional indigenous values:

> Colonial education in this country was therefore not transmitting the values and knowledge of Tanzanian society from one generation to the next: it was a deliberate attempt to change those values and to replace traditional knowledge by the knowledge from a different society. It was thus a part of a deliberate attempt to effect a revolution in the society; to make it into a colonial society which accepted its status and which was an efficient adjunct to the governing power. (Nyerere, 1968, p. 270)

At the time of Tanganyika's independence, there were few people with the necessary qualifications to strengthen the administration of government. The country was impoverished and the educational infrastructure was largely underdeveloped. It was a major effort to provide universal primary education, let alone secondary education for all. In fact, secondary schooling was provided for only a select few. It is for this reason that Nyerere argued that primary schooling should not be conceived of as a preparation for secondary schooling, since the majority would not benefit from the latter. The situation was rendered problematic by the fact that private secondary schools existed alongside state schools. These schools allowed those who could afford to pay for their education the chance of benefiting from secondary schooling (see Bacchus, 1973). Furthermore, with regard to state schools, it is an acknowledged fact (practically a truism), substantiated by a huge corpus of sociological research, that any process of selection based on 'meritocracy' in effect favours those with the greatest amount of resources and congenial *cultural capital*. In Tanzania's case, these were the children of those 'new elites' who, following independence, had obtained lucrative jobs in the civil service (ibid.). This situation must have had a deleterious effect on any attempt to create an egalitarian society (ibid.).

One of the major goals for Tanzania was the provision of universal primary education by the end of 1977. Pressure was placed on bureaucrats to expedite this process, the slogan being 'we must run while others walk'. As a result of this bold step, Tanzania witnessed a massive expansion in state education. Nyerere himself provides the following statistics:

> [A] tremendous jump in the number of children attending primary schools has been the result. In 1967 there were about 825,000 pupils in Tanzanian primary schools. In 1975 the comparable figure was 1,532,000 pupils, and the numbers will continue to rise rapidly for some years to come. (Nyerere, 1977, p. 8)

Nyerere also advocated an education which provided students with a sense of self-reliance, the focus being mainly on the development of an agrarian economy. It had to be an education characterized by the fusion of learning and producing, both processes taking place simultaneously. Each school had to develop its own means of subsistence. This concept is very much in keeping with the socialist tradition. One can cite as examples here: Marx's notion of a polytechnic education, as propounded in the Geneva Resolution of 1866 (see Castles and Wustenberg, 1979, cited in Livingstone, 1983, pp. 186, 187); Paulo Freire's advocacy of a fusion between education and production in his advice to the PAIGC leadership in Guinea Bissau (see Letter 11 in Freire, 1978, pp. 99–120); the introduction, in Malta, under Dom Mintoff's socialist administration, of the student-worker, worker-student and pupil worker schemes (5.5 month period of study alternating with a 5.5 month period of work) at sixth form and university levels; the system in China under Mao which involved a 2–4, 2–4 (2 months working-4 months studying, 2 months working-4 months studying) process (Chu, 1980, p. 79). The following statement by Mao best anticipates the spirit of the education-work process which Nyerere advocated:

> Whoever wants to know a thing has no way of doing so except by coming into contact with it, that is by living (practising) in its environment. (Mao, cited in Chu, 1980, p. 79)

The idea of school farms was developed in Tanzania: 'every school should also be a farm; that the school community should consist of people who are both teachers and farmers, and pupils and farmers' (Nyerere, 1968, p. 283). Nyerere also went so far as to stress that the pupils' welfare would depend on their farm's output very much the same way that the peasants' livelihood depends on the produce yielded by their land. (ibid.). Nyerere did not mince his words: 'by this sort of practice, and by this combination of classroom work and farm work, our educated young people will learn to realize that if they farm well they can eat well and have better facilities in the dormitories, recreation rooms, and so on. If they work badly, then they themselves will suffer' (Nyerere, 1968, pp. 284, 285). He even encouraged experienced farmers and agricultural officers to participate in the project:

> Life and farming will go on as we train. Indeed, by using good local farmers as supervisors and teachers of particular aspects of the work, and using the services of the Agricultural Officers and assistants, we shall be helping to break down the notion that only book learning is worthy of respect. This is an important element in our socialist development. (Nyerere, 1968, pp. 283, 284)

The school was no longer to be the exclusive domain of professionally formed teachers. In keeping with the idea of a productive community school, the entire community was to be regarded as a learning resource. This concept is quite in tune with the literature on community schools and the more progressive literature on parental and other community members' involvement in the education of children. It is a literature which underlines the importance of people outside the teaching profession having a say in the development of the school and contributing to the education it provides. In this respect, it is a literature which raises an important question: Who can effectively act as an educator within the community?

Nyerere maintained that it was absolutely vital that the schools and their pupils were to be integrated into village life: 'The children must be made part of the community by having responsibilities to the community and having the community involved in school activities' (Nyerere, 1968, p. 287). He suggests that school work – terms, times and so on – be organized in such a way that the children are allowed to participate, as family members, in the family farms, 'or as junior members of the community on community farms' (ibid.).

As far as school capital is concerned, Nyerere believed that school farms should derive no more assistance than would be available to an ordinary established cooperative farm where the work is supervised (Nyerere, 1968, p. 284). Through such means, the students could, according to Nyerere, learn the advantages of 'co-operative endeavour' especially 'when outside capital is not available in any significant quantities' (ibid.). Of course, the responsibility for upkeep was to be much stronger at secondary level than at primary level (Nyerere, 1968, p. 287). The problem, though, is that, according to a report published in the early 1970s, secondary schools were the least affected by the move to introduce farming in the schools (Bacchus, 1973). The report stated that the majority of secondary schools still placed their greatest emphasis on formal academic studies (ibid.). It also stated that, in primary schools, teachers with a very poor agricultural background placed emphasis on physical work on the farm, at times to the detriment of the 'educative' aspect of the experience (ibid.). In order to ensure that the primary school children were old enough to engage in running the school-farm, the educational authorities in Tanzania raised the primary school entry age 'from 5 or 6 to 7 years' (Kassam, 1994, p. 252).

Nyerere sought to provide an education which 'de-colonized the mind' to use a very popular term in Africa reminiscent of Frantz Fanon, Ngugi Wa Thiong'O and the former Cape Verde president, Aristides Pereira (with respect to the last mentioned, see Freire, 1985, p. 187). He states that the education provided must be 'for liberation', acknowledging that a 'liberated nation, in Africa or elsewhere, is not just a nation which has overcome alien occupation. That is an essential first part of liberation, but it is only the first. Liberation means more than that' (Nyerere, 1979c, p. 43). The country, as Aristides Pereira underlined with respect to Cape Verde, might have been de-colonized but now the task is to de-colonize the mind. For Nyerere, this meant that Tanzania had to become a 'self-reliant nation' while its people had to overcome feelings of inferiority and be able to use circumstances rather than be used by them (Nyerere, 1979c, p. 43). For Nyerere and others, however, such a decolonizing or liberating process entails a valorization of that which is indigenous. Kiswahili was established as the national language while educational institutions were to promote African culture. A firm believer in indigenous cultures, Nyerere states: 'No longer do our children simply learn British and European history. Faster than would have been thought possible, our University college and other institutions are providing materials on the history of Africa and making these available to our teachers' (Nyerere, 1968, p. 271). National songs and dances found their place in the postcolonial Tanzanian curriculum. Civics lessons gave secondary school pupils some understanding of the aims of the young Tanzanian state. (ibid.). Furthermore, a national board was introduced to set and mark examinations (Samoff, 1990, p. 209), a postcolonial measure adopted by a number of other former British colonies (see Bray and Steward, 1998).

It is not only schools that had to forge a link with the community but also the university. In a speech inaugurating the University of Dar es Salaam on 29 August 1970, Nyerere wrote: 'When determining whether a particular subject should be offered, the university should therefore be asking itself: "What contribution can a study of this subject make to Tanzania's future?" . . . "What knowledge of, or from, our own society is relevant to this matter?"' (Nyerere, 1979a, p. 41). The university was to provide materials for a genuinely postcolonial school curriculum, including materials in Kiswahili. While advocating the tailoring of university provision to the needs of the country, Nyerere still felt that the university must be allowed the freedom to experiment, to try out new courses and methods (Nyerere, 1979a, p. 42). He argued that the staff must pose challenging questions to the students and the university must pose challenging questions to society at large (ibid.).

As for students, Nyerere states: 'The peasants and workers of a nation feed, clothe, and house both the students and their teachers, they also provide all the educational facilities used – the books, test-tubes, machines and so on. The community provides these things because it expects to benefit – it is making an investment in people' (Nyerere, 1979a, p. 39). He even criticized the tendency among educated workers to place a price tag on themselves. In an address to the University of Liberia on 29 February 1968, Nyerere states: 'Shall we, in other words, use the skills which society has enabled us to acquire, in order to hold that same society to ransom?' (Nyerere, 1974, p. 7).

Of course, Nyerere, in a manner recalling Mao's reaction against Confucian principles and the Mandarin class, stressed that there should be no distinction between 'educated' and 'uneducated', between 'intellectual' and 'manual' labour. One of the most popular pictures of the former president is that in which he is shown wielding an axe in a *shamba*, in the company of other toiling peasants. It would be naïve to ignore the obvious PR element involved here, the sort of ploy adopted by many politicians and, in particular, *populist* politicians ever so eager to appear 'close to the people' or, more appropriately, 'the masses'. It ought to be underlined, however, that farming was the activity to which Nyerere returned following his retirement from Tanzanian politics.

Like Freire and others, Nyerere warned against intellectuals and 'experts' underestimating the knowledge of peasants and workers. He points to the fact that in Tanganyika, 36 million pounds were spent by colonialists on a Ground Nut scheme. It turned out to be an expensive failure since the 'experts' underestimated the knowledge of local farmers, who they dismissed as illiterate and so made their own decisions regarding rainfall regularity. They also assumed that it was simple indolence that made people reluctant to cut down all the trees when planting a *shamba*, 'So large areas were cleared – and few nuts grew, but erosion began!' (Nyerere, 1974, p. 10).

One area which was given a tremendous boost in Tanzania during Nyerere's presidency was adult education. Nyerere is a respected figure in the global adult education movement. Professor Budd L. Hall, former secretary general of the *International Council for Adult Education* and former head of the Department of Research, Institute of Adult Education, Dar es Salaam, wrote recently:

> Among his many accomplishments was his role as the founding Honorary President of the International Council for Adult Education. He delivered the keynote address to the First World Assembly of Adult Education organized in Dar es Salaam, Tanzania in June of 1976. His vision created the national slogan for 1970 Adult Education Year, 'Elimu Haina Mwiso' . . . Learning Never Ends . . . that was used on the commemorative cloth printed specially for the 1976 ICAE World Assembly.

That Nyerere is often cited in adult education circles is not surprising given his country's achievement of 'outstanding standards' (Bacchus and Torres, 1988, p. 322) in the area. Many of these achievements have been outlined in the literature (see, for example, Bhola, 1984; Hall, 1973a, 1973b; 1975; Hall and Kassam, 1972; Hall et al., 1972; M. Mayo, 1997; Sumra and Bwatwa, 1988; Unsicker, 1986). As Jeff Unsicker (1986) reports in his detailed study of Tanzania's literacy campaign, it was stated in Tanzania's first five year development plan that 'the nation cannot wait until the children have become educated for development to begin' (p. 231). As with the process of universal primary education, the feeling again was that 'we must run while others walk'. At the above mentioned ICAE World Assembly, Nyerere stated that adult education 'incorporates anything which enlarges' people's 'understanding, activates them, helps them to make their own decisions, and to implement those decisions for themselves' (Nyerere, 1979b, p. 51). One of the aims of adult education, as with all education, was to liberate the mind in a way that allows people to develop a strong sense of agency characterized by a belief in their ability to master circumstances. One of the major challenges for adult education, according to Nyerere, was to combat what he perceived as a traditional sense of fatalism among Tanzanian people:

> The importance of adult education, both for our country and for every individual, cannot be over-emphasised. We are poor and backward, and too many of us just accept our present conditions as 'the will of God', and feel that we can do nothing about them. In many cases, therefore, the first objective of adult education must be to shake ourselves out of a resignation to the kind of life Tanzanian people have lived for centuries past. (Nyerere, 1979d, p. 33)

The situation is similar to that described by Paulo Freire with respect to the oppressed of Brazil. 'They resort (stimulated by the oppressor) to magical explanations or a false view of God, to whom they fatalistically transfer the responsibility for their oppressed state . . . A Chilean priest of high intellectual and moral caliber visiting Recife in 1966 told me: 'When a Pernambucan colleague and I went to see several families living in shanties [*mocambos*] in indescribable poverty, I asked them how they could bear to live like that, and the answer was always the same: "What can I do? It is the will of God and I must accept it"' (Freire, 1970, p. 163).

It appears most appropriate that, at some stage, reference is made to Paulo Freire's ideas when discussing Nyerere's educational speeches or writings. Nyerere and Freire admired each other's writings, with the former having read *Pedagogy of the Oppressed* and the latter having been 'so impressed by the writings of Nyerere' that he told the Tanzanian president, on his visit to the latter's home 'on the outskirts of Dar es Salaam' in 1971, 'that he would like to organize a series of seminars where his speeches could be discussed and analysed in depth' (Hall,

1998, p. 97). The similarities between Nyerere's ideas and Freire's appeared so strong to the Brazilian educator that '[h]e asked President Nyerere to provide support for an educational centre in Tanzania based on the ideas of Freire and Nyerere,' a proposal which never materialized, although Freire, together with Moacir Gadotti, eventually managed to establish the Instituto Paulo Freire in São Paulo in the latter stages of the Brazilian educator's life (Hall, 1998, p. 98).

Arguably, the greatest similarity between Nyerere and Freire lies in their emphasis on listening to the learners and 'building on' the knowledge that they possess. It was important for Freire that one does not remain at the same level of knowledge (Allman et al., 1998, p. 11) and that the educator should be disposed to learn from the learner (Freire, 1970, p. 67; Freire, 1985, p. 177). With regard to the second point, Nyerere states:

> [E]very adult knows something about the subject he is interested in, even if he is not aware that he knows it. He may indeed know something which his teacher does not know. For example, the villagers will know what time of the year malaria is worse and what group of people – by age or residence or workplace – are most badly affected [*sic*]). (1979b, p. 53)

And yet, Michaela von Freyhold states, with respect to the Tanzanian literacy campaign, that these principles were not observed: 'After a visit by Paulo Freire to Tanzania there were some discussions on whether it would be advisable to make the primers more 'problem-posing' and open. In the end this suggestion was turned down. The planners argued: 'If we allow the peasants to criticize the advice of the extension agent, we undermine his authority' [*sic*]. Nor should there be any discussion of the choice of crops: 'If peasants begin to discuss whether they want to grow cotton or not they might decide against it, and if they produce no cotton where are we going to get our foreign exchange from?'

(von Freyhold, 1979, p. 166, cited in Unsicker, 1986, pp. 241, 242). Interesting strictures which raise the issue regarding the extent to which the imperatives of economic viability ran counter to the principles of a liberating education, a situation which was not unique to Tanzania (see Carnoy and Torres, 1990).

The immediate task, underlined by Nyerere, 6 years following the start of a much documented mass literacy campaign in Tanzania, is enabling adults to 'acquire the tools of development – the literacy, the knowledge of health needs, the need for improved production, the need to improve dwelling places and the basic skills necessary to meet all these needs' (Nyerere, 1979b, p. 55).

Important landmarks in the development of adult education in Tanzania were of course the setting up of the Institute of Adult Education at the University of Dar es Salaam, including an impressive correspondence school (Bhola, 1984, p. 154), and Kivokoni college, the latter being developed on the lines of England's Ruskin College (M. Mayo, 1997, p. 65). Ruskin College, a residential college for workers, fascinated Nyerere who 'invited one of the younger Ruskin organizers, Joan Wicken, to work with him in Tanzania' (Hall, 1998, p. 96). She eventually became 'President Nyerere's personal assistant and sometimes speech writer' (ibid., p. 97) and, together with the president, founded Kivokoni College (p. 96). Kivokoni College focused on providing 'political and ideological training of lower level government officials and party cadres in the regions' (Bhola, 1984, p. 154). Other colleges of this type were subsequently created in other zones of the country (ibid.). Of course, the extent to which this can be considered a genuine, critical political education or an exercise in partisan party indoctrination remains a moot point. Is there a fine line between the two?

The mass literacy campaign was a considerable success and won the Unesco Literacy Award. Key figures like Paulo Freire were associated, in an advisory capacity, with the campaign, although Freire's involvement in this particular instance has been described as 'peripheral' (Torres, 1982, p. 87). The literacy programme went on for many years, sustained by the ministry and other agencies, including the Swedish International Development Agency (SIDA) and the United Nations Development Program (UNDP) (Mushi, 1994, p. 67). As with most literacy campaigns, many of the thousands of teachers employed were volunteers who, according to Unsicker (1986), were trained in workshops and were paid a small honorarium of 30 shillings per month (p. 239) However, there were also primary schoolteachers who acted as adult educators (Mushi, 1994, p. 68). The usual problem in such instances, encountered also in other contexts, is that some of them replicate with adults the approaches they use with schoolchildren (Sumra and Bwatwa, 1988, p. 268; Mushi, 1994, p. 68). I also wonder, judging from my own experience as a former literacy coordinator in Malta, whether the use, as adult education centres, of primary schools (Mushi, 1994, pp. 67, 68), which have not been restructured or built in such a way that they accommodate community members of different ages, contributed to this replication. The process of mobilization in Tanzania involved various media including primers and radio broadcasts in a country where radio provided, in the rural areas, the only means of technological communication. There were also post-literacy programmes involving the study of a number of subjects. Even prior to the 1970 literacy campaigns, there had been Scandinavian influenced experiments based on folk education, often involving radio study groups in different rural areas (Unsicker, 1986, p. 234). Folk Development Colleges (FDCs), inspired by the Scandinavian (more specifically, Swedish) Folk High Schools, were also set up as residential colleges for those who had successfully been through the literacy programme and who were selected by their village communities to attend residential courses intended to be of benefit to the community at large (Bhola, 1984, p. 154; M. Mayo, 1997, p. 64). The FDC programme 'was launched in 1975' and has seen to the provision of 'courses for village leaders (chairpersons, secretaries, bookkeepers and village shop managers); leaders of women's organizations, household activities and small scale industries; various groups engaged in implementing various self-reliance projects; and assistant field officers' (Sumra and Bwatwa, 1988, p. 264). These FDCs have survived, judging from recent literature (Earth, 1998, p. 59).

All these developments placed Tanzania in the forefront of initiatives with regard to adult education in the 1970s. Certainly, many of the programmes depended to a large extent on foreign funding, a potentially contradictory situation, given that self-reliance was the declared goal. This funding diminished in the 1980s especially following the onset of neoliberal policies brought into place by such institutions as the IMF and the World Bank with their 'structural adjustment' programmes. There were disagreements between Tanzania and the IMF which remained unresolved until 1986. These disagreements concerned the IMF's 'insistence on sharp cuts in public spending', particularly 'in the social services' and on 'a substantial devaluation' (Samoff, 1990, p. 218). Tanzania has, since then, embarked on a path of development which can be regarded as a far cry from the policies advocated by Nyerere. There are those who would no doubt argue that his ideas were largely out of touch with a world governed by the imperatives of technological development and 'competitivity'. Others regard him to have been more of a philosopher king, confronting the logic of capitalist and neo-colonial development with alternative ideas rooted in indigenous forms of practice. There are those who underline the difficulties that confront a state such as Tanzania undergoing transition through non-revolutionary means (Samoff, 1990, p. 268).

In his last days, Nyerere often stated that he always carried with him two books, the Bible and the Arusha Declaration. This attests to Julius Kambarage Nyerere's lifelong commitment to Christian-socialist principles. These are principles to which even Freire adhered as I had occasion to remark earlier. The foregoing indicates that one can find several similarities between Nyerere's writings and those of Freire. One important point of contact would be the development of participatory action research in Tanzania through the efforts of Budd Hall, Yussuf Kassam and others. It was indicated earlier on that PAR draws heavily from Freire. These similarities can easily encourage a more systematic comparison between the two. I avoided this here but felt that such similarities were sufficient to justify an inclusion of a chapter on Nyerere in this volume reverberating with echoes from Freire.

FREIREAN INSPIRATION

CHAPTER 11

Critical Pedagogy, Historical Materialism and Dialectical Thinking: A Tribute to Paula Allman

When I left Paula Daryl Allman's house on the evening of Tuesday 25 October 2011, I felt this would probably be the last time I actually saw her, even though I was hopeful that I would get another chance; a tribute session was being planned for London early in the new year. The session was duly held on 4 February but Paula Allman was not to be there to experience the general appreciation of and indebtedness to her work. I did not expect her passing to occur so soon after my brief visit to Nottingham. She had appeared to be in good spirits, though understandably weak. Intellectually alert as ever, she had been following the financial fluctuations on Bloomberg TV. She explained that she avails herself of such opportunities to understand capitalism in order to be able to critique it. And the Afterword to the re-publication, in paperback, of her much cited *Critical Education Against Global Capitalism. Karl Marx and Revolutionary Critical Education* (Allman, 2010) indicates the extent to which she had been following developments connected with the crisis of capitalism, drawing on a range of sources to provide a detailed account, relating these developments to insights derived from her decades-old close reading, in English, of Marx's texts.

Allman's rigourous academic writing and teaching left a legacy in various parts of the world. As a child, she held national swimming records in the United States, thus being groomed for potential Olympic stardom. She could not fulfil her promise as a result of physical ailments and eventually taught swimming to adults. She taught at different levels of education in her country and graduated from Florida International University, with a doctoral thesis on Piaget. In 1973 she settled in England after having taken up a post-doctoral fellowship there. For years she was social science staff tutor for the East Midlands Region of the Open University and subsequently established herself at the University of Nottingham in what was the oldest adult education department in the United Kingdom. Her early writings included pieces on lifelong education (Allman, 1982), published in the very first issue of *International Journal of Lifelong Education*, on adult development (Allman, 1983) and also on the education of older adults (Allman, 1984), specifically a chapter which appeared in Eric Midwinter's *Mutual Aid Universities*. She once told me that she regarded herself, at the time, as a 'well intentioned liberal'.

Subsequently, she became very attracted to critical education inspired by the writings of Marx, of whose works she developed an impressive knowledge (one of very few people that I know who seem to have read Marx's large corpus, albeit in English translation, *in toto*), Gramsci and Freire. She wrote numerous articles on or inspired by these authors in a range of academic journals and edited books (e.g. Allman, 1999; 2002), some in collaboration with her colleague at Nottingham, John Wallis (Allman and Wallis, 1990, 1995a,b, 1997). She even coordinated a diploma and Master's degree course in the area inspired by the philosophy of Paulo Freire. She was also very active in social movements both in her native country and in Britain. She was the first co-chairperson for Nottingham CND and served in the education sub-group of The Socialist Movement. In my last conversation with her she mentioned how she got to know

E. P. Thompson as a result of the CND involvement and also befriended Caroline Benn whose husband, the former Labour MP, Anthony Neil Wedgwood 'Tony' Benn, wrote an endorsement for one of her books. She was closely connected with the Institute for Educational Policy, an independent educational radical Left policy unit, and collaborated with scholars such as Glenn Rikowski, Dave Hill, Mike Cole, Shahrzad Mojab, Peter McLaren, Helen Raduntz and Helen Colley. She served on the editorial advisory boards for *Convergence*, the journal of the International Council for Adult Education and Sense publishers' book series 'International Issues in Adult Education'.

Paula Allman continues to be revered by those who dream of and work towards ushering in a better world. She touched the lives of many persons. I was first touched by a 1988 essay of hers on Gramsci, Freire and Illich (Allman, 1988) in a book on radical adult education edited by Tom Lovett. The essay directly connected with my own research interests. It affirms the indebtedness of both Gramsci and Freire to Marx and specifically Marx's theory of consciousness in which the respective works of the Brazilian and the Sardinian are anchored. It focuses on the experience of adopting insights from the two authors in the course of the diploma in adult education programme she coordinated at the University of Nottingham. One aspect of Marx's approach which Freire develops in his *Pedagogy of the Oppressed* and which Allman underlines is the dialectical mode of conceptualization and writing which, as Allman indicates, is not easily accessible to readers schooled in conventional ways of thinking, often characterized by a linear approach.

I was eventually privileged to get to know her personally and to collaborate with her on conference and journal projects, also co-writing a couple of pieces with her. One of the pieces I co-wrote was an essay on Gramsci and Freire within the context of globalization, an essay which I presented on her and my behalf at the 1997 SCUTREA conference at Egham Surrey and which was subsequently included in the proceedings (Allman and Mayo, 1997). In that essay we drew on Gramsci's insights, from his notes on Americanism and Fordism, on capitalist reorganization and the falling rate of profit, to shed light on the intensification of globalization and its effects on education, specifically adult education. We used the word 'intensification' to emphasize capitalism's globalizing tendency since its inception. It was in fact Paula who alerted me to the quote from Marx and Engels' *Communist Manifesto*, reproduced at the outset of the SCUTREA essay, wherein it is stated:

> The need of a constantly expanding market for its products chases the bourgeoisie over the whole surface of the globe. It must nestle everywhere, settle everywhere, establish connections everywhere. The bourgeoisie has through its exploitation of the world-market given a cosmopolitan character to production and consumption in every country. To the great chagrin of Reactionists, it has drawn from under the feet of industry the national ground on which it stood. (Marx and Engels, 1998, pp. 7–8)

I had earlier formed part of a panel on Freire (with Sue M. Scott, Daniel Schugurensky [in absentia] and Elisabeth Lange) at the 1996 AERC meeting in Tampa, Florida, which was meant to include Paula Allman; she had to pull out because of a fall that exacerbated her back problems which plagued her certainly for as long as I knew her. I thus had the onerous task of presenting and doing justice to her piece on Freire entitled 'Freire with No Dilutions' (Allman, 1996), an obvious reference to the way his thinking is frequently distorted through liberal and *laissez-faire* appropriation. She contrasted his view of dialogical education with other contemporary views of learning through dialogue which she regarded as somewhat manipulative. She would later write about Freire's pedagogy:

> Freire argues that this [*his particular conception of dialogical education*] is a very different form of education. It begins with teachers having a different theory or concept of knowledge, which arises from and then exists in unity with a transformed relation to knowledge. And I can testify to the fact that when you take what he is saying seriously and try to apply it, you will experience the difference. It is a revolutionary-transformational-difference that acts as a catalyst for even more profound transformations. These . . . involve every participant in the learning group struggling to transform simultaneously the relation between teacher and students and each person's relation to knowledge. And, in so doing, they dialectically reunite the processes of teaching and learning within themselves. (Allman, 2001, p. 174)

I was eventually pleased to see her ideas and writings coalesce into four single-authored books: *Revolutionary Social Transformation: Democratic Hopes, Political Possibilities and Critical Education* (Allman, 1999), *Critical Education Against Global Capitalism Karl Marx and Revolutionary Critical Education* (Allman, 2008), *On Marx. An Introduction to the Revolutionary Intellect of Karl Marx* (Sense, 2008) and a revised and updated paperback version of *Critical Education Against Global Capitalism Karl Marx and Revolutionary Critical Education* (Sense, 2010).

There are many insights from these works that I derived for my own writing, much of which also benefited from comments provided by Paula when still in draft form. The issue of dialectics is that which, in my view, Allman explains brilliantly (Allman, 1999, 2002, 2008, 2010). The more one is familiar with Marx's 'tracking down' of 'inner connections' and 'relations', which are conceived of as 'unities of opposites', the more one begins to appreciate *Pedagogy of the Oppressed*'s Marxian underpinning (Allman, 1999, pp. 62–3). A thorough exposition is provided by Allman in her second book (Allman, 2001, pp. 39–48). The oppressed in Freire's conception but echoing Marx would be engaged in a struggle for humanization. In doing so, they would be engaged, in Marx's terms, in 'negating the negation', meaning the negation, in the latter sense, of the conditions for their ongoing humanization by those who are dehumanizing themselves as they dehumanize others (see Allman, 2001, p. 41).

Pedagogy of the Oppressed is not the only book Freire has written, but it is the most compact and consistent with regard to his dialectical conceptualization of power (Allman et al., 1998, p. 9), especially in its first three chapters; Freire had originally intended these three chapters to constitute the book (Schugurensky, 2011). The issue of dialectical thinking is elaborated in a collective piece to which I contributed, from which the quote in Chapter 8 is derived, but for which Paula Allman wrote the first draft. This piece served as the Editorial to a special issue of *Convergence* on Freire (a tribute issue published a year after his death), a journal on whose Editorial Advisory Board Paula Allman has served since the mid-1990s.

I would like to dwell at some length on Paula Allman's first book which was included in the critical education series edited by Henry Giroux and the late Joe Kincheloe for Bergin and Garvey, a series which was originally also edited by Paulo Freire himself. This book drew admiration from people outside the adult education field, notably people working in critical pedagogy and also historical materialism. Paula Allman's book came out at a time when we had been exposed to the misplaced triumphalism of capitalism that led many to think that 'what is' established the limits of 'what should and can be'. We were told that we are witnessing the 'end of history' by an author who, thankfully, subsequently modified his position. Some ludic forms of post-modernism would have us believe that the current historical conjuncture has brought an end to the 'grand narratives' (Allman and Wallis, 1995a). We were and still are confronted with a fatalism that is as insidious as it is nihilistic.

This scenario is borne in mind by Paula Allman in *Revolutionary Social Transformation*. Together with others in the same vein (Foley, 1999; McLaren, 2000; Youngman, 2000), she sets out to expose the inanity of the above claims. She indicates that the grand narrative of Marxian (i.e. belonging to Marx himself) thought has much to offer as we explore radical democratic possibilities for a life guided by a vision heralding the democratic resolution of the dialectical contradiction between oppressor and oppressed – to be seen not as binary opposites but as being in a dialectical relationship. The book centres on the ideas of three figures regarded by Allman as central to the proposed project of a 'revolutionary social transformation': Karl Marx, Paulo Freire and Antonio Gramsci. The last two figures require no introduction because they have long been among the key sources of reference in this regard. Marx, too, is a key source. However, with perhaps the exception of Youngman (1986) and a series of articles by W. John Morgan, rarely has his thought been given such comprehensive and detailed treatment in the English-language adult education literature as in this book and the two later books by Allman; in her introduction to Marx's revolutionary intellect (Allman, 2008), she even provides a long and detailed glossary of terms adopted by Marx often in very nuanced ways. Gramsci's and Freire's ideas are shown (rightly, in my view) to be firmly embedded in Marx's theory of consciousness and his related dialectical method of analysis. Both Gramsci and Freire make capitalism the focus of their analyses. That Gramsci is indebted to Marxian thought (even though many of Marx's early writings were not available to him) goes without saying (see Allman, 2002), given that the Sardinian is credited with having 'reinvented' some of Marx's concepts when analysing important features of Italy's post-Risorgimento state.

As for Freire, Allman demonstrates clearly that one cannot fully appreciate his thinking unless one roots it in Marx's dialectical conceptualization of oppression. Allman refutes the liberal bourgeois notion of equality and inclusion. Echoing Stuart Hall, she regards this as operating on only an abstract level because it was 'never intended to operate in our material experience' (Allman, 1999, p. 137). She questions whether it 'possibly could do so within capitalist social relations' (ibid, p. 137). She even refutes the fashionable malaise of 'relativism', which renders one perspective as valid as the other. In this respect, she would find support in Gramsci, who was always critical of relativism. Most memorable are the opening lines from his review of Luigi Pirandello's play *Cosi è se vi pare (so it is if you think so):*

> The truth in itself does not exist, it is nothing but the highly personal impression that each individual draws from a certain fact. This statement may be (indeed, certainly is) nonsense, the pseudo-wisdom of a wit who wants to score superficial merriment from incompetent listeners. (Gramsci, 1985, p. 81)

In response, Allman distinguishes between meta-transhistorical truths (e.g. 'human beings, for better or worse, create history'), transhistorical truths (which hold throughout history to date, but the situation can change in the future), historically specific truths and conjuncturally specific truths. Allman's vision for transformed democratic social relations is predicated on a pedagogical approach characterized by revolutionary as opposed to reproductive praxis (Allman and Wallis, 1990). Here, action, reflection and transformative action exist not in a sequential relationship but in a dialectical one. This pedagogical approach echoes Marx's dialectical conceptualization, reflected in Freire's writings. Teaching and learning are conceived as 'two internally related processes within each person' rather than as separate processes that find their respective embodiments in the teachers and learners of the bourgeois pedagogical relation. Knowledge is considered not static, as a 'thing' or 'commodity', but as a 'mediation or tool between people and the world which either helps or hinders a critical perception of reality' (pp. 97–8).

Paula Allman's book, as its sequel (Allman 2001, 2010), is a *tour de force*. It is rigourous, it provides deep knowledge of Marx, Gramsci and Freire, and it is inspiring in the use of these three figures' ideas to promote radically democratic social relations. Reference to this book and its sequel strikes me as being de rigueur for any writer on education wanting to engage the Marxist tradition. They continue to be cited. For instance, news of her death reached me as I was anonymously reviewing a manuscript, for a prominent critical sociology journal, in which the author or authors cited her work extensively – a remarkable but ultimately sad coincidence!

Critical pedagogy has lost one of its important figures but her legacy will live on among those students and colleagues whose lives she touched, and through her writings, scattered in various journals, edited volumes and three single-authored books, the first two forming a diptych.

Like many I will miss her scholarship and especially her deep and holistic understanding of Marx, Gramsci and Freire. I also admired her spirituality. Like Freire, she was a 'person of faith', something she refers to in her writing, specifically in the *Critical Education Against Global Capitalism* book. Above all, I will miss her deep, genuine friendship and her love for humanity and other species, including the pets (one of her dogs was named PK, for Paulo Freire and Karl Marx) which shared her space and which she adored. *Here was a woman who knew how to love.*

CHAPTER 12

Dissidence, Love and Cultural Power: An Essay on Antonia Darder

Antonia Darder represents one of the most powerful and passionate dissident voices in contemporary critical pedagogy. She was born into poverty in the US colony of Puerto Rico, with a turbulent upbringing and life of struggle that made her face, first hand, many of the issues she would later engage with in her large output of essays, academic research work, poetry, music and painting (see Darder, in Borg and Mayo, 2007; Darder, 2011a, 2011b). She espouses a critical pedagogy that is inspired by the work of Paulo Freire among a host of other writers. The Freirean echoes are so strong, reverberating throughout her oeuvre, and most especially a volume dealing exclusively with his ideas and inspiration (Darder, 2002), that an essay on her work is most appropriate in a book such as this.

Darder's struggles have involved juggling different contexts initially as a result of mandatory US policies such as 'operation bootstrap', which forced thousands of Puerto Ricans to move elsewhere. She was subsequently raised in east Los Angeles and she has faced key issues with regard to racism, poverty, class warfare and language policies that together provided the grist for her passionate and very perceptive writings and other forms of cultural production. These issues remain as pertinent today as they were at the time of her upbringing and formation as a public intellectual.

Besides being a scholar, Antonia Darder is an activist and visual artist, who has participated in a variety of grassroots efforts connected with educational rights, worker's rights, bilingual education, women's issues, environmental justice and immigrant rights. One of her major efforts as an activist occurred in the 1990s when she worked with teachers and community members to convene educators from across California to establish the *California Consortium of Critical Educators* (CCCE). This is a radical teachers' organization that espoused an educational vision of schooling intimately linked to social justice, human rights and economic democracy. More recently (2005), she established a radio collective with students and community members who produced *Liberacion!*, a public affairs radio programme on WEFT. She writes about this experience and the virtues of community radio as a source of alternative media (Darder, 2011a, 2011c), describing the way by which community radio can furnish public pedagogical spaces for often marginalized community voices. In so doing, emancipatory community radio challenges the narratives of wealthy representatives of capital and the corporate sector, who exert untold influence on the mainstream media. It also serves as a vehicle for developing community relationships and encouraging civic participation in the public sphere.

Darder's output is so varied that it also includes the production of an award winning documentary, *Breaking Silence: The Pervasiveness of Oppression*. It was based on a critical narrative study. The documentary analyses the persistence of inequality within the academy and its negative impact on the lives of underrepresented students. In addition, over the last 20 years, she has supervised nearly 100 PhD dissertations, mainly of working class students of colour. The completion rate for these students is 96 per cent. This, in my view, speaks volumes for the dedication she reserves for her students. And all this was carried out in addition to her activism and scholarly writings, both fully embedded in her lifelong struggles as a person and educator.

And yet all these vicissitudes including her movement through the educational system from community college to nursing to graduate school to finally becoming one of the most respected Leftist voices in the United States have enabled her to eschew the kind of identity politics that has led to what the Egyptian writer Nawal El Saadawi (1997) calls a postmodern 'divide and rule'. In this situation, the totalizing structure of an ever-globalizing capitalism is confronted by divisive politics among the grassroots, the point made earlier in the discussion on social movements. On the contrary, Darder focuses on the way capitalism serves as a totalizing force structuring different forms of entities on gender, ethnic and nationality lines with class having a strong transversal presence. Her writings and convictions in this regard ally her with such forceful writers as Ellen Meiksins Wood, whom she quotes approvingly on a number of occasions. Rather than reflecting on 'race' as some biological and therefore 'fixed' factor, she focuses, especially in her work with Rodolfo Torres (Darder and Torres, 2011a, pp. 93–108; Darder and Torres, 2008), on racism resulting from the process of racialization, which is part and parcel of the way the imperatives of capitalist production are satisfied and its segmentation of its global labour market.

> Racism represents one of the most violent forms of human oppression that exists in American society and yet, it seems one of the most difficult for most individuals of the dominant culture to comprehend. Often the difficulty arises in the faulty perceptions and assumptions that persist in the deeply hegemonic consciousness of most Euroamericans. In addition to strong ethnocentric values, much of the difficulty is related to a pervasive and commonsensical ideology of race coupled with a modernist worldview that effectively truncates the ability of most Euroamericans to move from an individual perception of bias and prejudice to an understanding of racism as a structural phenomenon associated with institutional power and control.

> This is particularly so when questions of inequalities are simultaneously tied to class oppression. (Darder, 2011b, p. 37)

In this regard she gives due recognition to the insights brought into the field of critical education by those who espouse 'critical race theory'. She argues that they made central the issue of 'race' in discussions on education 'as well as indigenous examinations of schooling, culture, and language'. However, given her critique of the use of 'race' as an essentializing biological category, she insists in a number of writings, not least an essay which appears in her edited volume of critical pedagogy (Darder et al., 2008), that she is more inclined towards the development of a critical theory of racism.

Given her own life struggles as a person whose first language is Spanish but who had to survive in an ethnocentric environment which privileged English and therefore resulted in a form of cultural invasion for immigrants from outside the United States and within official US borders, especially to the detriment of many Hispanics living in California, Darder attaches great importance to a critical theory of biculturalism. Once again, this issue remains pertinent today in several parts of the world, not least in the region (the Mediterranean) where I have been born and raised. This is because of the influx of immigrants not only from Eastern Europe but most particularly from North Africa and Sub-Saharan Africa. A critical bicultural education would be applauded by many dedicating their lives towards the inclusion and well-being of migrants in Italy, Malta, Spain and Portugal, to name just a few, and who adopt a critical emancipatory stance not always embraced by the many NGOs that have emerged as possibly the agents of a new 'technology of power' in this area. Ngoization makes its presence strongly felt with regard to migration. And yet the dominant hegemonic discourse in education, with its focus on bench-marking, standardization, league tables, buttressed by such opinions, from the likes of Angela Merkel and

David Cameron, that 'multiculturalism has not worked', militates against this kind of efforts.

Darder, drawing on her own experiences as a woman whose first language was not English but Spanish and who gradually struggled to become comfortable with both (her evocative and poetic writings in English attest to this), exposes the colonizing nature of these theories and processes which are the staple of such political forces as the English Only movement and the Tea Party in the United States. This colonizing approach resulted in such political developments as Proposition 227, California's anti-bilingual education stance; Proposition 203, Arizona's anti-immigration bill and Article 13, the measure devised in Colorado to deny services to undocumented immigrants (Estrada, in Darder, 2011b, p. 187). More recently we have read of measures to ban the use of non-American and especially Latino classics in Arizona schools. These are all measures which, in their colonial 'one shoe fits all strategy', render bicultural students grossly disadvantaged in the educational system. The situation recalls the legacy of direct colonialism in the country I come from where English is the dominant language as a result of which most Maltese students, who speak the native national-popular Maltese language in their homes and other milieus, are at a disadvantage. In our educational system, the colonial, albeit international hegemonic language, is the language of assessment. This applies from the early years of schooling. The need for a critical bicultural education is even more urgent in a world increasingly under the sway of what Macedo, Dendrinos and Gounari (2003) call the 'hegemony of English'. It becomes even more urgent as the legacies of colonialism and intensification of globalization, climate change and other factors, including indigenous ones, are leading the impoverished of ransacked Africa to seek new pastures, often in countries which should already accommodate a bicultural existence and which have changed from countries of emigration to countries of immigration.

Darder's drawing on a Freire-inspired critical pedagogy, which also benefits from the insights of other sources, makes the struggle for an emancipatory bicultural education more pressing. One cannot develop a critical pedagogy centring around the key notion of *praxis*, the key concept in Freire's philosophy, by embracing an education that is mono-cultural and that involves not the learners' first language but the dominant standard one. My own experience with Maltese students in situations such as these corroborates Ngugi Wa Thiong'O's (1986) view that the process of communication is mainly cerebral lacking the other dimensions that come into play when the first language is engaged. This in my view makes a mockery of praxis which entails coming into consciousness. As Marx and Engels (extensively engaged by Darder especially with regard to dialectical thinking) argue, language is 'practical consciousness' which is as old 'as consciousness itself' (Marx and Engels, 1970, p. 51). It recalls Freire's (1985) statement, with reference to Guinea Bissau's revolutionary leader, Amilcar Cabral: 'Language is one of culture's most immediate, authentic and concrete expressions' (in Freire, 1978, p. 184).

Darder's insists on a different way of working with teachers. This would entail engaging authentic aspects of the cultures of different students in a process which does not remain simply at that level (this has been one of the major critiques of multicultural experiences in education seen as a form of containment) and which allows students to learn effectively in both cultures, recognizing, as Freire would maintain, the ideological presence of the colonial language. This recognition should not be facile (colonialism has always been complex and the colonized have often been skilful in appropriating aspects of the dominant culture for their own ends). It would rather serve as a means not to allow subaltern learners to remain, as Freire and Gramsci would put it, at the margins of political life. In short it would allow them the means to exercise their 'right to govern'. This, in my view, would be an important requirement for a teacher education that emphasizes the politics of knowledge and learning and a genuinely democratic education. It has a wide international geographical resonance, extending beyond the United States.

With migration being a strong feature of the world as we know it and with the mental legacies of direct colonialism still present everywhere as a result of its colonization of the 'mental universe of the colonized' (Ngugi, 1986), a critical bicultural education, as propounded by Darder, remains most urgent. Early childhood educator Sharon Cronin was one of many teachers who worked with Antonia Darder in the area of critical bicultural education. Her voice as well as that of nine others are given space in the twentieth anniversary edition of *Culture and Power in the Classroom*. Cronin discusses what is called the *Soy Bilingue* (I am Bilingual) programme, conceived by Darder and her co-educators, and which resulted in a book documenting novel experiences in biculturalism.

Cronin states that, in writing the Foreword to the *Soy Bilingue* book, 'Darder introduced the metaphor of a ship without a rudder from one of José Martí's poems. It again serves us well in examining the role her work in bicultural development has played in steadfastly guiding our praxis in working with teachers in our community' (Cronin, in Darder, 2011b, p. 140). She went on to outline the core pedagogical components of the Soy Bilingüe Adult Dual Language Model that include: (1) Language and Literacy Development, (2) Collaboration and Community Building, (3) Cultural Relevancy and Active Teaching, (4) Imagination and Cultural Expression, (5) Bicultural Voice and Cross-Cultural Competency, (6) Critical Thinking and Conscientization and (7) Coaching and Accountability' (Cronin, 2008, p. 2, reproduced in Darder, 2011b, p. 140).

It should be an education that enables all learners to be *subject* (and not object) in the Freirean sense, one which transcends *assistenzialismo* (as the Italians would call it) and which embraces and engages with the standpoints of the learners' culture of origin, the key to their consciousness manifest in language. It also entails a 'productive pedagogy' for each and every member of the learning setting, one which contributes to the *collective* and individual growth of the students, that enables them to govern and come to terms with their contradictions, to be less incomplete.

In this regard, Darder's engagement with insights that derive from neuroscience and their emphasis on the plasticity of the brain (which calls into question culturally conditioned IQ tests) becomes most instructive for persons and communities conceived of as 'beings in process', very much in keeping with Freire's identification of the ontological task of human beings as being that of becoming more fully human.

> And what this research resoundingly demonstrates is the incredible *neuroplasticity* of the brain – the capacity for human beings to learn new information and construct new knowledge, throughout their lifetime . . . Thus, under optimal conditions, the brain of all human beings continues to develop, albeit at slower pace than the early years, but significantly, nonetheless. (Darder, 2011b, p. 72)

Emphasis is here placed on the cognitive and physical aspects of learning as well as the imagination, so well developed by Darder herself in her own literary output and given its due prominence in the work of Maxine Greene.

Much of the foregoing indicates a strong connection between Darder's work, especially that concerning language imposition, resistance and bicultural alternatives, and the field of postcolonialism to which she has made a very active contribution. A keynote speaker in recent years at the business meeting of the AERA's Postcolonial SIG, she has been serving as co-editor (with Anne Hickling Hudson and me) of Palgrave-Macmillan's book series on 'Postcolonial Studies in Education'. Coming from what is virtually a direct colony of the United States and being an *independentista*, Darder has a connection with the field that seems natural. Her writings on language imposition together with the imposition of other 'homogenizing standards' in education connect with the shape colonialism takes in a context such as the United States where colonial relations between nations get transposed through a process of structured racialization of different ethnic groups consisting of people originating from formal and informal colonies, not least those hailing from the informal Latin American colonies.

Antonia Darder is a prolific writer and editor of compendia (she even compiled a Latino Studies reader). I had the pleasure and honour to co-write a piece with her for *Counterpunch*, which grew out of a joint editorial preface we wrote on a book concerning Cuba. While we do not romanticize the Caribbean island and its revolutionary politics, we highlight some of the principles which governed the revolution and its educational policies (Darder and Mayo, 2011). I would argue that the principles governing these pedagogical politics would sit comfortably, at least as principles, if not in their implementation, with the philosophy that much inspired Freire's work; no wonder Freire was looking forward, at the time of his death, to receiving an award from Castro.

Darder is one of the leading exponents of Freirean pedagogy and a critical pedagogy more generally. In highlighting the main aspects of a critical pedagogy (Darder, 2007, 2011a,b), she places emphasis on the important notions of praxis, dialectical thinking (she gives due recognition to the late Paula Allman and her elaboration of this aspect), hegemony, the collective dimensions of learning and revolutionary love, the last mentioned with its echoes from Freire himself and such revolutionaries as Ernesto 'Che' Guevara. These principles are expanded, with insights from practising teachers, in her book *Reinventing Freire. A Pedagogy of Love*. Freire himself, whom she had met at a conference and with whose ideas she engaged in his presence, finding in his words some of the language she required for her own struggles (a language born in struggle), wrote a short but highly edifying preface to the first edition of *Culture and Power in the Classroom* and it is reproduced in the twentieth anniversary edition. He states:

> Antonia Darder's *Culture and Power in the Classroom* presents a passionate analysis of the pedagogical dimension of culture, particularly when she critically describes cultural experiences or the experiences of cultural subjects within a xenophobic context that too often treats difference with disrespect. Her book makes us confront the experience of cultural subjects that are not allowed to live a fully multicultural life in a society which is, by definition and make-up, multicultural. I say this with much conviction; I fear that most of these cultural subjects are living only a form of multicultural formality and not a substantive multicultural existence – to the extent that the U.S. cultural hegemony systematically relegates all forms of multicultural expression considered outside of the so-called 'common culture' to the margins. (Freire, in Darder, 2011b, p. 234)

It is in her book on Freire, however, parts of which are reproduced in the all embracing *A Dissident Voice*, that she highlights the notion of *love* (see also Darder, 2011a, ch. 9) that is to lie at the heart of any revolutionary pedagogy. We have seen in Chapter 2 how Freire regards love as being 'the foundation of dialogue' (Freire, 1970a, 1993, p. 89). Allman and Darder actually brought home to me the centrality of love as the basis of all good teaching and emancipatory work. For Antonia is not swayed by some of the most nihilistic strands of postmodernism as my earlier treatment of her writings on racism and the totalizing structuring force of capitalism will hopefully have shown. Her conception of education is one which is emancipatory. She states:

> [Freire] was thoroughly convinced that the process of dialogue, central to his pedagogical project, could not exist 'in

> the absence of a profound love for the world and for people'. . . . it was through such love, he surmised, that teachers could find the strength, faith, and humility to establish solidarity and struggle together to transform the oppressive ideologies and practices of public education. (2002, pp. 91–2)

It lies at the heart of Freire's notion of revolutionary struggle as manifest in many of his statements in interviews indicating how he would love to be remembered and which Paula Allman, as I show, highlighted in a joint tribute piece, written with me and others, soon after Freire's death, for which she wrote the first draft. Of all the gems from *Pedagogy of the Oppressed*, she selected the following, from the Preface, as title: 'a world in which it will be easier to love' (Freire, 1970a, 1993, p. 40; see Allman et al., 1998, p. 9), the sort of world to which Freire aspired to make a contribution.

Darder's book on Freire shuttles between the macro and micro levels. She views his ideas against the backdrop of the intensification of globalization and neoliberal policies. The voices of educators and cultural workers highlight the way these policies impact directly on people's lives. It also foregrounds the issue of courage that has to be shown by any meaningful educator who indulges in critical pedagogy as a way of life and not simply as some form of trendy radical chic. There is a price which has to be paid. Courage and paying the price have been features of Antonia Darder's life and educational praxis. She has taken sides on important social issues and has suffered both in and outside academia for doing so, often expressing her frustration, even in personal telephone conversations with me, at witnessing colleagues not prepared to 'walk the talk'.

Over the years, I have come to know Antonia personally even though most of our contact has been confined to e-mail exchanges and the odd telephone conversation. As co-editor of the Postcolonial Education book series, I have had the opportunity to observe her at close quarters (via electronic communication) soliciting manuscripts and encouraging authors, including first time book authors, to improve their texts. Here is a person who is ever so ready to be of service to others, a team player who believes in the collectivity of academic and socio-political endeavour. I too benefited from her very detailed edits to work I shared with her; her generosity knows no bounds.

Her notion of a critical pedagogy is an expansive one which takes on board some of the feminist and environmental critiques of earlier expositions of this approach to teaching and learning. Once again, she does this without indulging in a paralyzing identity politics and therefore without losing sight of the structuring 'totalizing' politico-economic forces at play. There is a strong sense of spirituality which runs throughout her writing and which has a strong ancestral element to it, a sense of place and roots. I wonder to what extent this can connect with her work on the brain. Events such as the day of the dead (2 November) resonate with her as it does throughout different Latino and other contexts steeped in a Catholic culture. I will never forget the intriguing and touching moment when I received a card from her marking the day of the dead. One other streak which runs through her work is the sense of yearning for the freedom of the body reflected in constant references to the kind of music with which she grew up, music very much connected with the subaltern and which has pedagogical resonance as a form of expression – release, resistance and counter-discourse – in a world characterized by constant forms of colonization and policing.

Hers is a critical pedagogy that combines cultural insight with a strong dose of political economy. It is a pedagogy that however embraces love, passion and spirituality, and which scours different sites of cultural practice that comes to fruition in the multi-varied and multi-sensual analysis Antonia Darder brings to her work.

CHAPTER 13

Striving Against the Eclipse of Democracy: Henry A. Giroux's Critical Pedagogy for Social Justice

When focusing on contemporary critical pedagogy, reference to the work of Henry Giroux is de rigueur. He is, after all, a founding figure in the critical pedagogy movement. A most prolific writer, Giroux explores resources of hope when, as indicated in a book title of his, democracy is being 'eclipsed' by a new 'authoritarianism'. This sense of hope is enhanced by the promise surrounding Obama's election to the US presidency, though the bulk of Giroux's recent work, which I will discuss in this essay, surrounds the years of G. W. Bush's terms in office.

Giroux has, however, already expressed deep concerns about the contradictions characterizing Obama's first months in power, most trenchantly in op. ed. columns on topics such as the politics of lying (Giroux, 2009a), violence in schools (2009b, 2010b) and the disruptive proto-fascist practices meant to undermine social reforms that the new president seeks to introduce (Giroux, 2009d). Most of these criticisms are captured in *Politics After Hope: Obama and the Crisis of Youth, Race, and Democracy* (Giroux, 2010a), where Obama is shown to be continuing many of Bush's educational policies (see also Giroux, 2009a). The US president is also criticized in another work (Giroux, 2010b) for promoting many of the illegal legalities the Bush administration adopted to subvert the Geneva Accords and other international laws forbidding torture and the violation of human rights.

The new authoritarianism which Giroux writes about, certainly in his 2004 book *The Terrors of Neoliberalism* (Giroux, 2004), and its revised version *Against the Terror of Neoliberalism: Politics Beyond the Age of Greed* (Giroux, 2008), makes its presence felt not only through figures in military uniform, visible though these may be in an age of increasing militarisation, but also through the all engulfing images of corporate power that characterize several aspects of our lives, comprising entertainment, youth culture, public schooling and universities. It is an authoritarianism that is or was mediated by a number of developments (see ch. 1 in Giroux, 2005a, pp. 30–108). These include:

- Neoliberalism – the state changes its traditional role, in this context, to one which provides the infrastructure for capital mobility and the repressive mechanisms to control those who react to their increasing marginalization in a system in which the market holds sway;
- the constant generation of a culture of fear, especially in the wake of 9/11 and other terrorist attacks;
- a strong sense of nationalism and patriotism – the creation of what Benedict Anderson calls an 'imagined community', in this case an imagined community of 'Americans' which often results in a culture of suspicion and a crackdown on dissent and anti-war activities and attitudes;
- an all pervasive presence of militarism, both abroad and at home, through a massive increase in incarceration of victims of neoliberal policies, policing of schools and a glut of images, including popular cultural images, which render militarization palatable and military enrolment attractive;
- a constant blurring of the traditional dividing line between religion (see ch. 5 of Giroux, 2006f) and state.

With respect to the last point, the war on the home front (authoritarian polices) and abroad was justified by a language that not only smacks of Orwellian 'doublespeak' (see ch. 7 in Giroux, 2006f) but was also couched in religious fundamentalist terms. In the recent G. W. Bush years, the situation was most pronounced even though such terms always formed part of the discourse pertaining to the conservative-neoliberal two-pronged strategy characterizing New Right politics – neoliberal economic approaches and conservative values.

This new authoritarianism is marked by a process of corporate encroachment in everyday life, very much a feature of the first mediation referred to earlier, the one concerning neoliberalism. Neoliberalism renders persons simply producers and consumers and not social actors who can engage in and help develop the public sphere and publicly and collectively challenge the forms of authoritarianism taking root.

Culture matters in this age of corporate encroachment, including the encroachment of the military–industrial complex, on our lives. I suppose it always mattered, as Antonio Gramsci underlined well over 70 years ago, emphasizing this dimension, alongside a political economic one, in his analysis of power and class politics in particular. Giroux, for his part, has been consistent in regarding the cultural sphere a key source of power, and he does this without eschewing important political economic considerations (although he is less remembered for this aspect of his analysis), and while perusing a variety of texts ranging from the print media to film. They all constitute forms of what he calls 'public pedagogy' (Giroux, 1999, p. 4). This concept best captures his attempt to extend the notion of pedagogy well beyond the important though very limited context of schooling. Every relationship of hegemony is an educational relationship, Gramsci would tell us, and, in this respect, Giroux engages a tradition that comprises the work of not only Antonio Gramsci (Giroux, 1980a, 1980b, 1988) but also Theodor Adorno, Raymond Williams, Walter Benjamin and more recently Stuart Hall, Paulo Freire, Michelle Foucault, Maxine Greene, Homi Bhabha, Noam Chomsky, Roger I Simon, bell hooks, Zygmunt Bauman, Judith Butler and Giorgio Agamben, to name but a few.

Giroux has always viewed the cultural terrain as a vehicle for the shaping of subjectivities and the cultivation of desires through a 'pedagogical' process, the structuring principles of which are political (Giroux and Simon, cited in Giroux, 1992, p. 188; Giroux and Simon, 1989, p. 10). It is also a vehicle for the production, enactment and circulation of social practices, to echo Stuart Hall (Giroux, 2000a, p. 9). As Gramsci had indicated, it is through culture that much, though not all, of the present hegemonic arrangements are developed and contested, given the incompleteness of these arrangements that allow spaces in which counter-hegemonic action can be waged (Giroux and Simon, cited in Giroux, 1992, p. 186; Giroux and Simon, 1989, p. 8).

Gramsci's importance in Giroux's thinking on the relationship between culture and power is reflected in the latter's early and later works. One of Giroux's earliest pieces is an article on Gramsci in *Telos*. The Sardinian Marxist politician and social theorist is the subject of illuminating essays by Giroux in later works such as *Stealing Innocence. Corporate Culture's War on Children* (Giroux, 2000b) and a paper that appears in both *Educational Theory* and an anthology of essays on Gramsci (Giroux, 2002). Giroux uses Gramsci and others to go beyond 'ideology critique', a situation which is a characteristic of contemporary German Marxist debates where Gramsci's ideas concerning hegemony are juxtaposed against the 'ideology critique' of the Frankfurt School.

Giroux draws on critical insights by Gramsci and others to help map out terrains in which people can act as social agents and 'transformative intellectuals' (Giroux, 1988) engaging 'in a commitment to a form of solidarity that addresses the many instances of suffering that are a growing and threatening part of life in America and abroad' (Giroux, 1997a, p. 104). It is a form of solidarity that highlights the *collective* dimensions of knowledge, one that 'emerges from an affirmative view of liberation that underscores the necessity of working collectively alongside the oppressed' (ibid.).

It is for this reason that he is critical of the position of certain academics who limit themselves to questions of textuality, ideology critique and signification (Giroux, 2000a, pp. 131–2). In his view, they would refrain from linking this work to the greater task of furnishing us with the anticipatory utopian vision of a radical democracy, characterized by equity and social justice.

These concerns emerge quite clearly in such later works as *The Mouse That Roared. Disney and the End of Innocence* (1999), *Impure Acts* (Giroux, 2000a), *Stealing Innocence. Corporate Culture's War on Children* (Giroux, 2000b), *Public Spaces/Private Lives. Beyond the Culture of Cynicism* (Giroux, 2001), *The Terrors of Neoliberalism* (Giroux, 2004), *Against the New Authoritarianism. Politics after Abu Ghraib* (Giroux, 2005a), *Take Back Higher Education* (Giroux and Giroux, 2004) and *Against the Terror of Neoliberalism: Politics Beyond the Age of Greed* (Giroux, 2008), to which I will devote the bulk of the attention in this chapter.

These books will together provide the springboard for a discussion of related themes broached in such works as *Disturbing Pleasures* (Giroux, 1994a), *Fugitive Cultures* (1996), *Pedagogy and the Politics of Hope* (1997a), the co-edited anthology, *Education and Cultural Studies: Toward a Performative Practice* (Giroux and Shannon, 1997), *Channel Surfing: Race Talk and the Destruction of Today's Youth* (Giroux, 1997b), besides *Stormy Weather. Katrina and the Politics of Disposability* (Giroux, 2006c) and *Beyond the Spectacle of Terrorism* (Giroux, 2006e).

As I had occasion to remark in a review essay on some of them (Mayo, 2002), these books mark the latest phase of Henry Giroux's work. The corpus of his work is indeed massive, with other works being completed at the time of my writing this book (articles concerning torture and articles on Obama's initial years as US president and the neo-conservative and new-authoritarian legacies he is expected to confront). Giroux's early works include a review of Paulo Freire's *Pedagogy of the Oppressed*, in *Interchange* (an academic journal that comes out of Canada), that led to a long-standing collaborative relationship between him and the Brazilian educator.

Giroux states that, when a high school teacher in the early 1970s, he discovered, in *Pedagogy of the Oppressed*, the language he required to justify his classroom pedagogical approach.

This approach was intended as an antidote to the 'barren', 'regimented', 'militaristic' schooling of the times; Giroux's alternative approach had been questioned by the school's vice principal (Giroux, 2006b). Giroux's tremendous respect for Paulo's work is pretty obvious given that essays on the Brazilian educator feature regularly throughout the American writer's oeuvre including an essay in *Stealing Innocence* and another on Freire and postcolonialism, in *Disturbing Pleasures*, that had originally appeared in an anthology of essays on Freire (McLaren and Leonard, 1993) and is reproduced in a recently published Giroux reader (Giroux, 2006a). Giroux found, in Freire's work, 'an attempt to take seriously the relationship between education and social change, to dignify the subject of learning, to be attentive to questions of contextualisation, to link education to particular forms of individual and social empowerment' (Giroux, 2006b, ch. 4).

According to Giroux, Freire's pedagogy, which was 'forged in a kind of struggle to link education to justice', remains relevant in this day and age. It provides the antithesis to the dominant education policy that characterizes the new 'authoritarianism' in the United States with its 'militarism', 'market fundamentalism' and a 'horrible religious fundamentalism that has nothing to do with genuine religious compassion and insight' (ibid.).

Giroux sees, as many do, this religious fundamentalism (ch. 5 in Giroux, 2006f) as co-existing, almost naturally, with the kind of authoritarianism that he inveighs against. It must be said that Freire's pedagogy too has religious overtones but which are mostly linked to the social justice–oriented 'Prophetic Church', the church that is linked to grassroots struggles against Empire, in Hardt and Negri's (2000) sense, and which is closely linked to Liberation Theology.

Giroux regards it as a pedagogy that does not 'see schools as merely testing centres' (ibid.). One notices shades of Don Milani and the boys of Barbiana here with their denunciation, in the *Lettera*, of the public school, the school that promotes the rich and 'figli di papa' (daddy's children, Scuola di Barbiana, 1996). Giroux considered Freire a model to 'link the political and the personal' (ibid.), which goes against the grain of contemporary hegemonic thinking through which issues are reduced to a matter of individual concerns and deficiencies while citizenship is, once again, defined in production and consumption terms (Giroux, 2006c, 2006d).

Giroux recognizes that Freire continues to serve as a resource that has consistently nourished his work as an educationist from the very beginning. Giroux's early works comprise writings that engaged the then dominant sociological theories of social/cultural reproduction and resistance in education, very much inspired by neo-Marxist writings (Giroux, 1981a, 1981b, 1983, 2006a). *Theory and Resistance* (Giroux, 1983) was regarded as a key text in critical pedagogy. As a matter of fact, there are those who continue to associate Giroux's name and style of writing exclusively with this text. In doing so, they fail to do justice to Giroux's large oeuvre, thus overlooking the evolution of his thinking and writing style over a 26-year period.

Giroux later collaborated with sociologist Stanley Aronowitz in roughly the same area (Aronowitz and Giroux, 1985).

Giroux drew a lot from the reproduction/production/resistance paradigm and, in his own words, engaged and continues to 'engage the Marxist tradition' (Giroux, 1992, p. 13). À la Gramsci, he also strove to add a 'critical cultural politics' (Giroux, in Torres, 1998, p. 136) dimension to the neo-Marxist educational paradigm, mining, in the process, such resources as Paul Willis' classic ethnographic work (*Learning to Labour*) and many others, notably the writings of key Frankfurt School figures, especially, as in the case of Adorno, work relating to the emancipatory phase rather than that belonging to the later 'negative dialectics' period. Adorno continued to remain a source of reference even in Giroux's recent work (Giroux, 2005a) that includes reflections on human rights violations in Guantanamo Bay and Abu Ghraib. Reference is made, in this Canadian text, to Adorno's celebrated essay: 'Education After Auschwitz'.

Giroux continues to engage the historical materialist tradition even in his most recent work, eschewing any kind of theoretical prescription and seeing it as a tradition that constantly requires extension and revitalization (Giroux, in Torres, 1998, p. 153) rather than a body of work to be regarded as some kind of 'ideological church'. It is a theme to which he returns in recent work as he expresses his concern that the Left requires a new language in these troubled authoritarian times:

> As the Right wages a frontal assault against all remnants of the democratic state and its welfare provisions, the progressive Left is in disarray. Theoretical and political impoverishment feed off each other as hope of a revolutionary project capable of challenging the existing forces of domination appears remote. (Giroux, 2005b)

Earlier, he had found the work of the reproduction theorists to be instructive but limited in its explanatory power and this led him to mine and draw critical insights from the area of cultural studies. German Marxist philosopher Ernst Bloch was an important source of influence, through his three-volume *Principle of Hope* (cf. Bloch, 1995). Certain strands of postmodern literature also made their presence felt in a number of works in which popular culture was conceived of as an important area of enquiry (Aronowitz and Giroux, 1991; Giroux and McLaren, 1989; Giroux and Simon, 1989).

In addition to these areas, one notices the influence of feminist literature (Giroux, 1991), postcolonial studies (1992) and post-structuralism, the last mentioned comprising the work of Michel Foucault. These influences continue to inform his work, though at no stage is the emancipatory element and the struggle for social justice missing from Giroux's writings.

Giroux's dissatisfaction with some of the excesses of certain post-modernist strands – their nihilistic, ludic and de-politicized posturing – drew him even closer to cultural studies, which enabled him to 'recover the primacy of the political' (Giroux, in Torres, 1998, p. 137). In many of Giroux's writings, the engagement with cultural studies is intensified (Giroux and Giroux, 2004):

> Culture not only mediates history, it shapes it. We argue that culture is the primary terrain for realizing the political as an act of social intervention, a space in which politics is pluralized, recognized as contingent, and open to many formations. (p. 95)

Giroux sought to bring a strong cultural studies dimension into the discourse on education and provide a pedagogical dimension to cultural studies itself. He feels that this approach is important to help revitalize the democratic public sphere. This emerges most clearly in a number of writings (see Giroux and Shannon, 1997). He has also been editing, for a number of years, an academic refereed journal intended to combine educational and pedagogical matters with cultural studies – *Review of Education, Pedagogy and Cultural Studies*. He shares this task with his wife, Susan Searls Giroux.

What renders cultural studies so important to education, in Giroux's eyes, is the fact that it deals with a whole range of pedagogical agencies. Quite evident here is Gramsci's influence, reflecting the Sardinian's influence on the now defunct Birmingham School of Contemporary Cultural Studies, recently given as much importance by the *Fondazione Istituto Gramsci* as Gramsci's influence on the relevant areas of subaltern studies and postcolonial studies.

These 'public pedagogical' agencies constitute the terrain where hegemony is both shaped and challenged. It can be challenged by virtue of an oppositional discourse, a discourse of transgression (a form of 'living dangerously', see Giroux, 1993) occurring 'in and against' institutions such as universities (Giroux and Giroux, 2004) and the film industry (Giroux, 2002), none of which are monolithic. Educators can avail themselves of these sites of struggle, in the shaping of desires, sensibilities and subjectivities, to act as cultural workers, transformative intellectuals and oppositional public intellectuals. These intellectuals act not alone but in solidarity with others. Their collective knowledge and actions presuppose specific visions of public life, community, and moral accountability (Giroux, 2000a, p. 141).

How can educators respond to the challenge posed by Giroux when advocating the adoption of a cultural studies approach to teaching/learning in various settings (see for instance Giroux and Giroux, 2004)? One way of ensuring that the cultural studies area becomes a meaningful political pedagogical practice, and not a 'radical chic' enclave, is by extending it to adult and community education/action. As Raymond Williams reminds us (Williams, 1993, p. 260), adult education provided the setting for cultural studies to emerge in its British versions.

For Giroux, adult education would be just one among many other settings for cultural studies and education, the latter conceived of in its widest sense. The terrain in which education takes place is broad enough to comprise a variety of pedagogical sites, sites that extend beyond the system of formal education. As a result, educational activity is engaged in by not only professional teachers and academics but a broader array of cultural workers that includes journalists and op-ed columnists, community activists and animators, architects, advertisers, photographers, artists, actors, film directors, social activists, religious ministers, musicians and so forth.

This partly explains why Giroux gradually moved from writing about public schooling to engaging in lengthy discussions of broader social issues, such as war and corporate power, and various forms of cultural production such as film, cartoons and media news packages. This represents a marked contrast to Giroux's early work around schooling. Public pedagogy occurs through a plethora of sites and means. The shift in Giroux's focus is also represented biographically by his move from a graduate school of education to the English and Cultural Studies Department at McMaster University in Hamilton, Ontario, Canada, where he holds a chair in Communication Studies.

Many of Giroux's works provide critical analyses of the broader pedagogical function of several important cultural sites, characterized by an increasing degree of corporate encroachment. In *Stealing Innocence*, he targets, as object of criticism and analysis, corporations such as Calvin Klein (Giroux, 2000b, pp. 74–81), a corporation that had already featured in *Channel Surfing* (Giroux, 1997b). In the same book, where some of the analysis of corporations echoes the earlier work focusing on Benetton adverts (Giroux, 1994a, 2006a), and chapter 9 of *America on the Edge* (2006f), he provides an incisive analysis of the loss of innocence occurring through such forms of 'anticipated adulthood' and thwarted childhood as child beauty pageants (Giroux, 2000b, pp. 39–64). These pageants also occur in our part of the world, as I have discovered from my 'teaching practice' supervisory duties in Malta.

Giroux's later work is also well known for its trenchant analyses of one of America's 'sacred cows', the Disney Empire (*The Mouse That Roared*).

This and related texts by Giroux (a synoptic version of the book's argument in a chapter in *Impure Acts*) aroused mixed feelings among some of the graduate students at my home university with whom I discussed the work. Many of the students made it clear that they consider Disney as one of their childhood's key sources of 'innocent pleasure'. Giroux's exposure of the insidiousness of the corporate, imperialist and hegemonic agenda, veiled by the spectacle of innocence and make-believe (see contrast with other forms of terrorism in Giroux, 2006e), must have come down on these learners, gripped by childhood nostalgia, as a cold shower. In this book, Giroux reveals the extent of Disney's corporate empire. The study combines cultural criticism with a dose of political economic analysis. This constitutes an interesting feature of this and other works by Giroux, given that he and other critical pedagogues and cultural theorists have often been accused of cultural reductionism. In Giroux's Disney analysis, we come across insightful and revealing episodes such as those exposing ruthless, asymmetrical management–labour relations in the Disney theme parks.

Giroux has written extensively on the film industry, which, as an essay, entitled 'Breaking into the Movies. Film as Cultural Politics' indicates, has provided a lifelong fascination (Giroux, 2006f). In fact his books are replete with chapters involving film criticism that constitutes an important feature of his oeuvre. The films covered include not only the numerous Disney blockbuster cartoons (which naturally figure prominently in *The Mouse That Roared*) but also, to name but a few, such films as:

- *Dirty Dancing* in a co-edited compendium of writings (with Roger I. Simon) on education and cultural studies (Giroux and Simon, 1989);
- *Dead Poets Society* (Giroux, 1993);
- *Boys 'n the Hood* and *Juice* (Giroux, 1994b, 2006a);
- Two Disney-Touchstone films, *Good Morning Vietnam* and *Pretty Woman*, in the *Mouse That Roared* (Giroux, 1999, pp. 129–30) and earlier work (1994a);
- *Fight Club* in *Public Spaces/Private Lives* (Giroux, 2001).

Giroux demonstrates how some of the images projected in these films serve, as with other images projected by different cultural products (e.g. adverts), as public pedagogies (Giroux, 2001, p. 75). These pedagogies resonate with broader social and political issues. This resonance has a bearing on the construction of our subjectivities, sensibilities and political dispositions. They would include such elements as:

- the racist misrepresentations of Arabs and the Orient (in Said's terms) in *Aladdin*;
- degenerate images of youth in 'heroin chic' adverts and such films as *Dangerous Minds*, *The Substitute I* and *High School High* (Giroux, 2000b, 2006a);
- racially discriminating overtones in the language of *The Jungle Book*;
- sexism in *Pretty Woman*;
- violence and machismo in *Fight Club*;
- the complex set of representations in black films of the 1990s, such as *Boys 'n the Hood* and *Juice*.

While revealing the sense of hopelessness and self-destructiveness that characterizes black neighbourhoods, *Boys 'n the Hood* and *Juice* feed into what Giroux regards as the US national stereotypical obsession with nihilism as being endemic to black youth culture. This set of representations provides little indication of the structuring forces at play, of which white middle-class American audiences are an integral part (Giroux, 2006a, 105–8).

Henry Giroux's comprehensive analysis comprises the scouring of different sources of pleasure and public pedagogy to drive home his central thesis: a war is being waged against children and youth (especially marginalized and 'disposable' youth such as blacks, indigenous and working class youth). The war is being waged against precisely those people who, in Giroux's view, should hold out the promise of a better future. Youths and children are made the subject of relentless attacks that take several forms, including coercion, demonization, militarization and commodification (through corporatist encroachment) within a New Right scenario. These themes feature prominently in his later works notably his latest *Youth in a Suspect Society. Democracy or Disposability?* (Giroux, 2009c).

Among the hardest hit, in Giroux's view, are undoubtedly the children and youth of those countries that are the victims of senseless wars waged by the United States and its allies targeting civilians (notably in Afghanistan and Iraq) and who die in their thousands, or are permanently maimed, through what is perversely dubbed 'collateral damage', a term which returned to haunt Americans in the trial connected with the Oklahoma bombing. Giroux's numerous writings on the subject are overwhelming in terms of the presentation of data indicating the deaths and injuries suffered by youth and children as a result of not only bombardments by US forces and their allies but also the indirect effects of the destruction of public infrastructure in Iraq, in the 1991 Gulf War, which led to malnutrition and deadly diseases (Giroux and Giroux, 2004, p. 70):

> As globalisation and militarization mutually reinforce each other as an economic policy and a means to settle conflicts, wars are no longer forced between soldiers but are now visited upon civilians, and appear to have the most detrimental effects on children. Within the last decade, 2 million children have died in military conflicts. Another 4 million have been disabled, 12 million have been left homeless, and millions more have been orphaned. (pp. 75, 76)

This recalls Don Milani and his students' denunciation of the use of poisonous gas by the Italian fascist army on Ethiopians, a denunciation which occurred in the midst of the students' search for a 'just war' which, they concluded, never existed (Milani, 1991). The above quote, from Henry Giroux and Susan Searls Giroux, refers to a situation brought about by the military–industrial complex that has rendered militarism the solution to world disputes caused, in part, by unequal access to the world's resources.

These wars, particularly those couched as 'wars on terror', provide legitimacy to stringent social measures and Orwellian 'Big Brother' surveillance strategies on the home front. This is all in the interest of pushing through neoliberal policies. Market relations, deregulation, consumerism and privatization are privileged at the expense of state interventions to safeguard social inclusion and solidarity. These latter elements become dirty words and those who cannot produce and consume are left to flounder by the wayside in a manner that was shockingly revealed to the world at large in the wake of Hurricane Katrina.

> Defined primarily through a discourse of 'lack' in the face of the social imperatives of good character, personal responsibility, and hyper-individualism, entire populations are expelled from the index of moral concerns. (Giroux, 2006d)

The situation, as Giroux drives home time and time again, is compounded by the emergence of a carceral state, an elaboration on Foucault's notion of a 'carceral society', that spends more on prisons, to discipline or 'weed out' the victims of such neoliberal policies, than on public education. Giroux shows, in common with such writers as Chomsky and Macedo, how there are more black youths in prisons than in public education institutions – a shocking revelation that attests to a war on children and youth being waged not only in Afghanistan and Iraq but also on the home front.

> Punishment, incarceration, and surveillance have come to represent the role of the new state. One consequence is that the implied contract between the state and citizens is broken, and social guarantees for youth as well as civic obligations to

> the future vanish from the public agenda. (Giroux and Giroux, 2004, p. 74)

One ought to remark that carceral states await the victims of neoliberal policies worldwide, notably countries that are serving as 'first port of call' for immigrants from Africa and Asia fleeing poverty, starvation (exacerbated by structural adjustment programmes) and internal wars fuelled by a potent Western based arms industry (the United States is the major exporter of arms, Giroux reminds us). The carceral settings awaiting such hapless victims include detention centres, euphemistically called, in Italy, centres of temporary 'hospitality', where immigrants are kept for long periods as they await decisions regarding whether they should be allowed in as refugees or repatriated. Neoliberal policies make their presence felt in these contexts since the provision of a grossly underpaid 'reserve army' of immigrants, including illegal immigrants, serves to depress local wages.

Needless to say, young people, mainly youth and children, feature prominently in this reserve army, with many people of their age having lost their lives in the process of crossing over from, say, the shores of northern Africa to southern Europe, in small and hardly durable dinghies and other vessels. They are often forced, at gun point, to jump off the boats, miles off the shores of a southern European country, and swim the rest of the distance, irrespective of whether they can do so or not. Drowning occurs frequently. Between July and September 2006, no less than 8,849 clandestine immigrants landed in Italy: 168 were discovered dead while 144 were dispersed. The Spanish newspaper *El Pais* reported that 490 bodies of immigrants were recovered from the African and Spanish shores. The same newspaper reports that the *Red Cross* and *Mezzaluna Rossa* believe that the number of clandestine migrants who have disappeared amounts to between 2,000 and 3,000 (ANSA, Madrid 28 August 2006; indebted to Melita Cristaldi for this information).

With regard to the link between Iraq and the United States, Giroux demonstrates how the massive cost of financing the war in Iraq is borne by the US people themselves since this is partly made good by cutbacks on the social wage that results in lack of funding for social programmes, including public education programmes, public health schemes and so forth. The brunt is thus borne by the poor who, once again, are treated as disposable beings: the 'human waste disposal' segment of American society, to use Zygmunt Bauman's words (Bauman, 2006). What renders the burden heavier is the fact that the Bush administration unabashedly provided the wealthiest segment of US society with huge tax cuts as part of its 'economic stimulus' policies (Giroux and Giroux, 2004, p. 80).

> While $723 billion dollars are allocated for tax cuts for the rich, state governments are cutting a total of $75 billion in health care, welfare benefits, and education. (Ibid., p. 59)

Giroux therefore demonstrates, throughout numerous works (Giroux, 2004, 2005a, 2006a, 2008; Giroux and Giroux 2004), that a war on the poor and disenfranchised is being fought on two fronts, the foreign and home front. In the latter case, it takes the form of '. . . the silent war at home' in that:

> [T]he Iraq war and the war against terrorism are being financed from cuts in domestic funding on health care, children's education, and other public services. (Giroux and Giroux, 2004, p. 57)

The Slovenian cultural critic Slavoj Žižek is quoted as having asserted that the 'true target of the "war on terror" is American society itself – the disciplining of its emancipatory excesses' (in Giroux and Giroux, 2004, p. 57).

The post-Katrina images provide testimony to the 'silent' war being waged on the home front, in which youth and children feature among the greatest casualties (Giroux, 2006c,d). The places that were hardest hit later became the target of militarization, for the prevention of looting, and social engineering. They also began to serve as laboratories for market reforms (Giroux, 2006c, p. 59). These reforms generally lead to gentrification, as a number of international experiences have shown. This situation is, according to Giroux, symptomatic of a new *biopolitics* devoid of 'democratic principles, practices and values and scornful of the social contract' (Giroux, 2006c, p. 63), the kind of contract one expects Obama to begin to observe, especially given his pledges in this regard.

Sites of public pedagogy continued to provide legitimacy for such nefarious polices, especially through the politics of representation of destitute youth underlying the unsavoury images referred to earlier (see Kellner, 2001, p. 143). These demonization strategies justify cuts in spending on youth welfare and other social programmes.

The war on children occurs, however, not only through the 'dismantling of the welfare state, but also through the pervasive glut of images that cast them as the principal incitements to adult desire'. This is the case of the child beauty pageants, the commodification of young female bodies, referred to earlier, which, in certain cases, can result in tragic deaths at the hands of paedophiles (Giroux, 2000b, p. 63). The war is waged on several other fronts.

For instance, the war on black youth, who feature among the greatest casualties of this onslaught, is discussed in several places, notably *Fugitive Cultures* (1996) and, as indicated, more recent work (Giroux, 2006a, ch. 6). The operative phrase in this context is 'zero tolerance' (Giroux, 2001, ch. 2). The whole theme of the carceral state relates to this notion, and what makes the situation worse is that black youth are often the target of an entire range of recruitment strategies, also involving popular culture devices, to swell the ranks of the military waging war both at home and abroad. Joining the military represents for such youth a way out of poverty, a way out which alas often leads to a similar dead end, a literal 'dead' end as the frequent images of body-bags, being returned from Iraq, reveal.

The situation of repression is compounded by the advent of a new McCarthysm having made its presence felt throughout US society (see Giroux and Giroux, 2004, ch. 1) and which spread to the universities, with professors being named in lists such as 'the dirty dozen' list and represented as people posing a threat to national security. Giroux's one time close colleague at Oxford-Ohio, Peter McLaren, featured prominently in this list. So did other collaborators such as Douglas Kellner. Even a revered deceased intellectual, Edward Said, was not spared such treatment given his influence on the suddenly 'dangerous' areas of middle eastern and postcolonial studies.

Giroux's discussions concerning the war (in many cases, class-based, sexist, homophobic and racist) being waged on youth and children have a strong international relevance. Racism, to provide an example, is undoubtedly a global reality (see Macedo and Gounari, 2006). Immigrants and their offspring are constantly being 'otherised' in a variety of countries that are increasingly becoming multi-ethnic. They are often depicted as potential terrorists especially in the wake of 9/11/2001 (New York and Washington), 3/11/2004 (Madrid) and 7/7/2005 (London). I would include here Malta, my home country, and other southern European states, including Italy. These countries have turned from net exporters to net importers of labour power (see Borg and Mayo, 2006; Mayo, 2004). They feature among the countries outside whose shores the tragic and at times clinical disposal of human lives, in the form of drowning migrants, to which I referred earlier, takes place.

The war on children and youth is often rendered palpable through acts of violence meted out to students in schools. I refer, in this context, to Giroux's recent op-ed on the brutalization of kids in schools. Special reference is made to the alleged beating of a 15-year-old disabled African American schoolboy, by a police officer, for not having tucked in his shirt (Giroux, 2009b).

The war is even more subtle and takes on a less blatant form. As Giroux indicates time and time again, it also comprises corporate culture's encroachment on all spheres of life. Capitalism constantly extends its reach in the quest for new markets and to draw more aspects of our existence into capitalist social relations of production. Public goods are converted to consumer goods, with citizenship being, once again, reduced to a two-dimensional aspect of our lives. From potentially social actors (see Martin, 2001, p. 5) engaging in the public sphere and availing ourselves of 'public time', the slowing down of time 'in order to question what Jacques Derrida calls the powers that limit "a democracy to come"', we are constantly reduced to being persons engaged in 'corporate time', that is '. . . a notion of accelerated time in which the principle of self-interest replaces politics and consumerism replaces a broader notion of social agency' (Giroux and Giroux, 2004, p. 227). In the latter case, everything is carried out at speed and with technical efficiency, allowing little time for deep reflection and therefore praxis.

While Giroux has extended his areas of analysis beyond schooling, he has not ignored the ongoing corporatization of schools and universities. On the contrary, higher education has become one of Giroux's favourite themes in his recent writings. This is understandable given the massive changes being brought about in these institutions. It is common knowledge that these changes are shaking the European university context (see Mayo, 2009) as a result of such developments as the so-called Bologna process intended for European qualifications harmonization purposes (Confederation of EU Rectors' Conferences and Association of European Universities, 2000; EC, 2007).

Many of Giroux's later works devote ample space to the issue of corporate encroachment in formal education. Henry Giroux expresses concerns regarding the way corporations (including Disney) trade advertising rights in the schools' rest places and corridors for funds. These concerns should be heeded by educators and school principals/heads in other countries. They might be willing to adopt 'quick fix' solutions in order to make up for cash shortages caused by neoliberal policies. Giroux's discussions concerning the university's corporatization are also instructive. The marketplace ideology and a technical rationality are taking precedence, in these institutions, over concerns with providing the tools for active citizenship in a participatory democracy in which people learn and develop the knowledge to exercise their 'right to govern' – to become sovereign citizens, in Don Milani's terms.

The commodification of higher education (see also ch. 6 of Giroux, 2006f) is manifest in a variety of ways:

- through increasing bureaucratization;
- the erosion of the humanities;
- the transformation of schools of education into places where one learns 'what works' rather than places where one engages in critical reflection;
- the transformation of the role of university presidents and deans from that of academic leader to that of a CEO;
- the exaltation of the notion of 'entrepreneurship', one of the major buzz words in recent university parlance;
- rendering university research dependent on corporate funding with ramifications for intellectual property and dissemination of results;
- instrumental knowledge gaining preference over other forms of knowledge that promote critical thinking.

Universities are increasingly becoming glorified training agencies evaluated for their contributions to the economy rather than for their contribution to the creation and revitalization of democracy (Giroux and Giroux, 2004, 2007). Giroux also underlines that they are increasingly becoming an important component of the 'military–industrial–academic' complex (Giroux, 2007).

Universities and other institutions of higher education have been undergoing changes that reflect the corporate world's preference for accelerated time in lieu of that sense of 'public time' that was once associated with schools and universities as public spaces that provided the right setting for reflection and assimilation – echoes of Don Milani's 'pedagogia della lumaca' (the pedagogy of the snail). These are some of the many issues raised by Giroux and his co-authors/editors in a number of works (e.g. Giroux and Giroux, 2004).

Given the increasing corporatization and commodification of what were once important public spaces, it is heartening to see that there are public and specific intellectuals who seek ways and means of extending their roles as educators outside the university. They forge alliances with activists and popular educators in different social sectors. In doing so, they face the risk of missing out on opportunities for career advancement since community involvement is rarely rewarded in department reviews or research assessment exercises. Quite laudable are the initiatives by academics to engage the academy in popular education, in such projects as the Ontario-based project WALL (Work and Lifelong Learning) or the Edinburgh-coordinated Popular Education Network, to select two examples from a number of initiatives (see the various contributions to Thompson, 2000). These initiatives allow educators, in and outside the academy, to become, in Giroux's terms, 'border crossers' (Giroux, 1992).

As border crossers, academics act beyond the traditional contours of their work to join forces with others to help generate a substantive democracy, regarded by Giroux, Freire and others as a *dynamic* and an *ongoing* process. Giroux's own predilection for writing about the themes of his books in the accessible media, from newspapers in Canada such as *The Toronto Star* to the online *In these Times* or *Truthout.Org* (he is a regular contributor) as well as his provision of video interviews accessible on such widely diffused internet sites as YouTube, is an indication of his efforts to walk the talk in engaging as a public intellectual. Following Pierre Bourdieu and others, he recommends this role, for university based academics and other intellectuals, in many of his works.

One also ought to highlight the very accessible and almost journalistic language in which most of his works are written, in contrast to his very early *Theory and Resistance* book. This strikes me as an important point to make given that critical pedagogy is often criticized, indiscriminately, for its obscure and 'esoteric' language that renders it far removed from the language of social activists, teachers and other cultural workers operating 'in the trenches'. Giroux is wary of romanticizing 'the trenches', so to speak, where one can easily lapse into the kind of 'tried and tested' routine activities without opportunities for reflection for transformative action. This brings to mind Socrates' well-known dictum, from the *Apologia*, that an unexamined life is a life not worth living, a dictum that is echoed throughout various undergraduate education classes.

As far as academics are concerned, they too are not to be romanticized, according to Giroux, who is well aware of the presence of several intellectuals adopting positions that ultimately do not challenge the status quo. Much has been written on this aspect of academic life where the lure of prestigious and lucrative 'technicist' career opportunities can easily lead academics to go with the flow of corporatization and academic entrepreneurship, buying into the dominant ideology that renders industry the panacea for the survival and relevance of the university. One need therefore not rehearse the literature. One ought, however, to refer to two types of intellectuals, among the many targeted by Giroux in his writings. There are those who appropriate Left wing revolutionary figures by providing domesticating (mis) readings of their works to reinforce conservative or at best non-threatening liberal positions regarding schooling and other social aspects. In chapter 4 of *Stealing Innocence*, Giroux engages in a damning criticism of E. D Hirsch's (mis)use of Antonio Gramsci's views with regard to schooling. Mario Alighero Manacorda had regarded these views as constituting an epitaph by Gramsci for a school that was but cannot be any longer since the social context has changed. The problem, according to the Sardinian intellectual, was that the new reforms introduced by the Fascist Minister Giovanni Gentile, at the time, represented a retrograde step and not an improvement with regard to the 'old' school (Manacorda, in Gramsci, 1972, p. XXIX). Like the essays on Freire and Hall, in the same book, Giroux's essay on Gramsci that builds on his earlier criticism of Harold Entwistle's position regarding Gramsci's Unitarian School offers us some very important theoretical insights intended to enhance the analysis of the very context-bound chapters in the book's first section.

Giroux is also scathing in his criticism of the type of intellectual who, in Foucault's terms, confines his or her leftist posturing to 'trading in polemics', a form of what Giroux regards, echoing a favourite phrase from Marcuse, as 'scholarshit':

> Lost here is any attempt to persuade or convince, to produce a serious dialogue. All that remains are arguments buttressed by an air of privileged insularity that appear beyond interrogation, coupled with forms of rhetorical cleverness built upon the model of war and unconditional surrender, designed primarily to eliminate one's opponent but having little to say about what it means to offer alternative discourses to conservative and neo-liberal efforts to prevent the democratic principles of liberty, equality, and freedom from being put into practice in our schools and other crucial spheres of society. (Giroux, 2000a, p. 14)

Cynicism and nihilism are rife in today's world and often generate a culture of derision directed at any attempt to drive home the point, stressed throughout the World Social Forum, that another world is possible. This nihilism and cynicism reflect a politics devoid of hope. Giroux argues for a politics of hope in the manner of such other radical intellectuals as Paulo Freire and Zygmunt Bauman.

Giroux advocates not a messianic hope but an 'educated hope' based on a critique of the present. This educated hope should, according to Giroux, be characterized by ongoing critique and renewal. In Freire's words, it should involve a process of 'annunciation' and 'denunciation' for a more radically democratic public sphere, where democracy, pedagogy and human agency are connected (Giroux, 2001, p. 125). Viewed this way, Giroux's vision is utopian. His is an anticipatory utopia, prefigured not only by critique of the present, in which he illustrates how the public sphere is being eroded through various means, including corporate and TV induced mass hysteria and a general critical illiteracy (Giroux, 2009d, 2009e), but also by an alternative pedagogical/cultural politics underscoring 'issues of value, ethics, meaning, and affect' (2001, p. 139).

He further goes on to echo his colleague and former co-author, Stanley Aronowitz, in calling for the emergence of a third party, a radical party, in the United States that promotes a new bio-politics, and a multifaceted politics at that, which 'must not only address the concerns of the middle classes but must also join with "rank and file" activists of trade unions, women's organisations, environmental and ecology movements, various factions of the freedom movements for Blacks, Latino/as, Asians, and other oppressed peoples, and the anti-war and global justice movements to expose the illusion of democracy in the United States' (Giroux, 2006c, p. 67). Freire's insights on the nature of the relationship between party and movements – the party should approach them without trying to take them over (Freire, in Escobar et al., 1994, p. 40) – strike me as being most pertinent and instructive in this context.

Giroux calls for more than this. He calls for an 'Oppositional Global Politics' based on an assessment of the emergence of the different forms of oppositional movements emerging in various parts of the world not least the emerging Centre-Left governments in Latin America (Giroux, 2000e, p. 81).

As I have shown, the sources mined by Giroux are many. This is what one expects from such a prolific writer. Popular culture features prominently in his analyses. As I stated once before (Mayo, 2002), however, it would be great, in future, to see such an analyses of popular culture complemented by work focusing on the way cultural production, associated with dominant social groups, impinges on popular sensibilities and offers spaces for critical appropriation. This would be truly gramscian. Pierre Bourdieu's work on distinction, *Distinction: A Social Critique of the Judgment of Taste*, becomes most relevant here.

I also indicated that, when analysing such corporate institutions as Disney, in books on the lines of *The Mouse That Roared*, readers should be provided with a sense of the way the institution is not monolithic. It is not sufficient, in my view, to reserve just one or possibly two paragraphs, in a book containing almost 200 pages, to acknowledging that this institution has its contradictions and 'progressive' and 'enterprising elements' (Giroux, 1999, pp. 26, 27). One expects a longer discussion on these contradictions and enterprising elements, with illustrative examples. This would enable us to see how these institutions can really be conceptualized as sites of struggle in a process of hegemony that, as Gramsci and others, notably Stuart Hall, have underlined, is never complete. In tennis parlance, one should therefore avoid trying to win games '6- love, 6-love'.

Henry Giroux's corpus is vast and varied and is characterized by different stages in the evolution of his thought. The amount of writing is overwhelming and one develops the sense that similar issues are constantly being developed, expanded and revised across a number of books that represent a specific stage in the development of his oeuvre. His works no doubt represent a bleak picture of the times in which he wrote much of his later work, in which a 'new fascism', predicated on religious fundamentalism and the 'passion of the Right', and the formulation of global military and local surveillance strategies, were no longer nascent but firmly entrenched. This is an integral part of the scenario which Obama had to face in his tenure of office.

This notwithstanding, Giroux's writings are, like those of Paulo Freire and Zygmunt Bauman, governed by a sense of hope. It is the hope of one whose work is motivated by the belief that another world is possible. Like Bourdieu, Giroux conveys the view that the purpose of the intellectual is to move beyond merely interpreting the world and raising different questions about it, to joining forces with others to help generate the right climate, through a long social, political and cultural struggle, to bring this other world about. In this regard, his work provides a welcome reprieve from the cynicism and nihilism that characterize a lot of the contemporary literature. These cynics and nihilists frequently pour scorn on any attempt to revitalize the emancipatory tradition in social theorizing, the tradition which Giroux revitalizes while clinging to it steadfastly. In this regard, he comes close to Freire whose influence he recognizes and whom he regards as the key figure in critical pedagogy.

Bibliography

Allman, P. (1982), 'New Perspectives on the Adult: An Argument for Lifelong Education', *International Journal of Lifelong Education*, Vol. 1, No. 1, pp. 41–51.

— (1983), 'The Nature and Process of Adult Development', in M. Tight (ed.), *Education for Adults: Adult Learning and Education*, Vol. 1, (pp. 107–23). London: Croom Helm.

— (1984), 'Self-Help Learning and Its Relevance for Learning and Development in Later Life', in E. Midwinter (ed.), *Mutual Aid Universities*, (pp. 72–89) Beckenham, Kent: Croom Helm.

— (1988), 'Gramsci, Freire and Illich: Their Contribution to Education and Socialism', in T. Lovett (ed.), *Radical Adult Education – A Reader.* London: Routledge.

— (1994), 'Paulo Freire's Contributions to Radical Adult Education,' *Studies in the Education of Adults*, Vol. 26, No. 2, pp. 144–61.

— (1996), 'Freire with No Dilutions', in H. Reno and M. Witte (eds), *37th Annual AERC Proceedings*, Tampa, FL: University of Florida.

— (1999), *Revolutionary Social Transformation Democratic Hopes, Political Possibilities and Critical Education*, Westport, CT: Bergin and Garvey.

— (2001), *Critical Education Against Global Capitalism. Karl Marx and Revolutionary Critical Education*, Westport, CT: Bergin and Garvey.

— (2002), 'Gramsci's Contribution to Radical Adult Education', in C. Borg, J. A. Buttigieg and P. Mayo (eds), *Gramsci and Education*, Lanham, MD: Rowman & Littlefield.

— (2004), 'Introduction', in C. Thake Vassallo and C. Vassallo (eds), *The Communist Manifesto. Marx's Legacy to Humanity*, Malta: University of Malta Press.

— (2008), *On Marx. An Introduction to the Revolutionary Intellect of Karl Marx*, Rotterdam and Taipei: Sense Publishers.

— (2010), *Critical Education Against Global Capitalism. Karl Marx and Revolutionary Critical Education*, Rotterdam and Taipei: Sense Publishers.

Allman, P. and Mayo, P. (1997), 'Freire, Gramsci and Globalisation: Some Implications for Social and Political Commitment in Adult Education', in P. Armstrong, N. Miller and M. Zukas (eds), *Crossing Borders Breaking Boundaries – Research in the Education of Adults. Proceedings of the 27th Annual SCUTREA Conference*, London: Birkbeck College University of London.

Allman, P. and Wallis, J. (1990), 'Praxis: Implications for 'Really' Radical Education', *Studies in the Education of Adults*, Vol. 22, No. 1, pp. 14–30.

— (1995a), 'Challenging the Postmodern Condition: Radical Adult Education for Critical Intelligence', in M. Mayo and J. Thompson (eds), *Adult Learning Critical Intelligence and Social Change*, Leicester: NIACE.

— (1995b), 'Gramsci's Challenge to the Politics of the Left in "Our Times", *International Journal of Lifelong Education*, Vol. 14, No. 2, pp. 120–43.

— (1997), 'Commentary: Paulo Freire and the Future of the Radical Tradition', *Studies in the Education of Adults*, Vol. 29, No. 2, pp. 113–20.

Allman, P., Mayo, P., Cavanagh, C., Lean Heng, C. and Haddad, S. (1998), Introduction. '. . . the Creation of a World in Which It Will Be Easier to Love', *Convergence*. Vol. XXI, Nos 1 and 2, pp. 9–16.

Althusser, L. (1971), *Lenin, Philosophy and Other Essays* (B. Brewster, trans.), New York and London: Monthly Review Press.

Apitzsch, U. (1995), 'Razzismo ed Atteggiamenti Verso gli Immigrati Stranieri. Il Caso della Repubblica Federale Tedesca', *Quaderni dei Nuovi Annali*, University of Messina, 33.

Apple, M. W. (2004), *Ideology and the Curriculum* (3rd edn), London and New York: Routledge.

Arnove, R. F. (1986), *Education and Revolution in Nicaragua*, New York: Praeger.

Aronowitz, S. (1993) 'Freire's Radical Humanism', in Peter McLaren and Peter Leonard (eds), *Paulo Freire. A Critical Encounter*, New York and London: Routledge.

Aronowitz, S. and Giroux, H. (1985), *Education under Siege, The Conservative, Liberal and Radical Debate over Schooling*, South Hadley, MA: Bergin & Garvey.

— (1991), *Postmodern Education*, Minneapolis, MN: University of Minnesota Press.

Bacchus, M. K. (1973), 'Report on Recent Educational Developments in Tanzania', Edmonton: University of Alberta.

Bacchus, M. K. and Torres, C. A. (1988), 'Framework for a Comparative Study of Adult Education Policy Implementation in Mexico, Tanzania, and Alberta', *The Alberta Journal of Educational Research*, Vol. 34, pp. 320–9.

Batini, F. (2008), 'Competenze e diritto all' apprendimento', in F. Batini and A. Surian (eds), *Competenze e diritto all'Apprendimento*, Massa: Transeuropa.

Bauman, Z. (2005), *Liquid Life*, Cambridge: Polity Press.

— (2006), 'The Crisis of the Human Waste Disposal Industry', in D. Macedo and P. Gounari (eds), *The Globalization of Racism*, Boulder, CO: Paradigm.

Betto, F. and Freire, P. (1986), *Una Scuola Chiamata Vita*, Bologna: E.M.I.

Bhola, H. S. (1984), *Campaigning for Literacy. Eight National Experiences of the Twentieth Century, with a Memorandum to Decision-Makers*, Paris: UNESCO.

Bloch, E. (1995), *The Principle of Hope* (3-volume set), Cambridge, MA: MIT Press.

Bonanno, P. (2002), 'The Process of Learning', in C. Bezzina, A. Camilleri Grima, D. Purchase and R. Sultana (eds), *Inside Secondary Schools. A Maltese Reader*, Malta: Indigo Books.

Borg, C. and Mayo, P. (2006), *Learning and Social Difference. Challenges for Public Education and Critical Pedagogy*, Boulder, CO: Paradigm.

— (2007), *Public Intellectuals, Radical Democracy & Social Movements. A Book of Interviews*, New York, NY; Frankfurt: Peter Lang.

Borg, C., Cardona, M. and Caruana, S. (2009), *Letter to a Teacher. Lorenzo Milani's Contribution to Critical Citizenship*, Malta: Agenda.

Bourdieu, P. and Passeron, J. C. (1990), *Reproduction in Education, Society and Culture* (2nd edn), London; Newbury Park, CA and New Delhi: Sage.

Bray, M. and Steward, L. (eds) (1998), *Examination Systems in Small States. Comparative Perspectives on Policies, Models and Operations*, London: Commonwealth Secretariat.

Brine, J. (1999), *Undereducating Women: Globalizing Inequality*, Milton Keynes: Open University Press.

Bruss, N. and Macedo, D. (1985), 'Toward a Pedagogy of the Question: Conversations with Paulo Freire', *Journal of Education* (Boston), Vol. 167, pp. 7–21.

Burtchaell, J. T. (ed.) (1988), *A Just War no Longer Exists. The Teaching and Trial of Don Lorenzo Milani*, Notre Dame, IN: University of Notre Dame Press.

Carnoy, M. and Torres, C. A. (1990), 'Education and Social Transformation in Nicaragua, 1979–1989', in M. Carnoy and J. Samoff (eds), *Education and Social Transition in the Third World*, Princeton, NJ: Princeton University Press.

Castles, S. and Wustenberg, W. (1979), *The Education of the Future: An Introduction to the Theory and Practice of Socialist Education*, London: Pluto.

Centre for Higher Education Policy Studies (CHEPS) (2007). *Towards a Cartography of Higher Education Policy Change. A Festschrift in Honour of Guy Neave*, Enschede: CHEPS, University of Twente.

Chu, D. (1980), *Chairman Mao. Education of the Proletariat*, New York: Philosophy Library.

Commission of the European Communities (CEC) (2000), 'Commission Staff Working Paper. A Memorandum on Lifelong Learning', Brussels: European Commission.

— (2003), Communication from the Commission. 'The Role of the Universities in the Europe of Knowledge', Brussels: European Commission.

— (2006), Communication from the Commission to the Council of the European Parliament. 'Delivering on the Modernisation Agenda for Universities. Education, Research, Innovation'. Brussels: European Commission.

Confederation of EU Rectors' Conferences and Association of European Universities (2000), The Bologna Declaration. 'On the European Space for Higher Education. An Explanation', ec.europa.eu/education/policies/educ/bologna/bologna.pdf, accessed on 23 November 2008.

Cronin, S. (ed.) (2008), *Soy Bilingüe Model for Early Childhood and Elementary Teacher Education*, Seattle, WA: Center for Linguistic and Cultural Democracy.

Dale, R. and Robertson, S. (2004), 'Interview with Boaventura de Sousa Santos', *Globalization, Societies and Education*, Vol. 2, No. 2, pp. 147–60.

Darder, A. (2002), *Reinventing Paulo Freire. A Pedagogy of Love*, Boulder, CO: Westview Press.

— (2007), 'Critical Pedagogy', in W. Hare and J. P. Portelli (eds), *Key Questions in Education*, Halifax: PhilEd Books.

— (2011a), *A Dissident Voice, Essays on Culture, Pedagogy and Power*, New York and Frankfurt: Peter Lang.

— (2011b), *Culture and Power in the Classroom*. Twentieth anniversary edition, Boulder, CO: Paradigm.

— (2011c), 'Radio and the Art of Resistance: A Public Pedagogy of the Airwaves', *Policy Futures in Education*, Vol. 9, No. 6, pp. 696–705.

Darder, A. and Mayo, P. (2011), 'Reflections on the Blockade, a Tricontinental Vision, and the Capacity to Share. The Promise of Cuba', *Counterpunch*, Weekend Edition, 7–9 October 2011, www.counterpunch.org/2011/10/07/the-promise-of-cuba/.

Darder, A. and Torres, R. (2004), *After Race: Racism After Multiculturalism*, New York: New York University Press.

— (2008), 'Shattering the Race Lens. Toward a Critical Theory of Racism', in A. Darder, M. P. Baltodano and R. D. Torres (eds), *The Critical Pedagogy Reader* (2nd edn), New York and London: Routledge (also published as Chapter 5 in Darder, 2011a).

Darder, A., Baltodano, M. P. and Torres, R. D. (eds) (2008), *The Critical Pedagogy Reader* (2nd edn), New York and London: Routledge.

Dekadt, E. (1970), *Catholic Radicals in Brazil*, Oxford: Oxford University Press.

Dewey, J. (1938), *Experience & Education*, New York: Collier Books.

Earth, B. (1998), 'Participatory Research. Gender and Health in Rural Tanzania', *Convergence*, Vol. 31, pp. 59–68.

EC (2007), 'From Bergen to London. The Contribution of the European Commission to the Bologna Process', Brussels: European Commission.

Elias, J. (1994), *Paulo Freire: Pedagogue of Liberation*, Malabar, FL: Krieger.

El Saadawi, N. (1997), *The Nawal El-Saadawi Reader*, London: Zed Books.

Elsheikh, M. (1999), 'Le omissioni della cultural italiana', in I. Siggillino (ed.), *L'Islam nella Scuola*, Milan: Editore Franco Angeli.

English, L. and Mayo, P. (2012) *Learning with Adults. A Critical Pedagogical Introduction*, Rotterdam and Taipei: Sense Publishers.

Escobar, M., Fernandez, A. L. and Guevara-Niebla, G. (with Freire, P.) (1994), *Paulo Freire on Higher Education: A Dialogue at the National University of Mexico*, Albany, NY: SUNY Press.

Fabbri, F. and Gomes, A. M. (1995), 'La mia pedagogia: Paulo Freire risponde a professori e studenti bolognesi', in M. Gadotti, P. Freire and S. Guimarães, *Pedagogia: dialogo e conflitto* (B. Bellanova and F. Telleri, eds) (pp. 92–103), Torino: Societa` Editrice Internazionale.

Fallaci, N. (1993), *Vita del Prete Lorenzo Milani. Dalla parte dell'ultimo*, Milan: Biblioteca Universale Rizzoli.

Fanon, F. (1952), *Black Skin, White Masks*, London and Sydney: Pluto Press.

— (1963), *The Wretched of the Earth*, New York: Grove Press.

Figel, J. (2006). 'The Modernisation Agenda for European Universities'. Ceremony of the 22nd Anniversary of the Open University of the Netherlands, Public Talk.

Fischman, G. (2009), 'Review of Peter Mayo, Liberating Praxis. Paulo Freire's Legacy for Radical Education and Politics', *International Studies in Sociology of Education*, Vol. 19, Nos 3 and 4, pp. 257–60.

Fisher, W. and Ponniah, T. (eds) (2003), *Another World Is Possible. Popular Alternatives to Globalization at the World Social Forum*, London: Zed Books; Nova Scotia: Fernwood Publishers; Kuala Lumpur: SIRD; Cape Town: David Philip.

Foley, G. (1999). *Learning in Social Action: A Contribution to Understanding Informal Education*, London: Zed Books.

Fondazione Laboratorio Mediterraneo (ed.) (1997), *Obiettivi e Mezzi per il parternariato Euromediterraneo. Il Forum Civile EuroMed*, Naples: Magma.

Freire, P. (1970a, 1993), *Pedagogy of the Oppressed*, New York: Continuum

— (1970b), *Cultural Action for Freedom*, Cambridge, MA: Harvard University Press.

— (1973), *Education for Critical Consciousness*, New York: Continuum.

— (1974), 'Authority versus Authoritarianism', Audiotape, *Thinking with Paulo Freire Series*, Sydney: Australian Council of Churches.

— (1978), *Pedagogy in Process: The Letters to Guinea Bissau*, New York: Continuum.

— (1985), *The Politics of Education*, South Hadley, MA: Bergin and Garvey.

— (1993), *Pedagogy of the City*, New York: Continuum.

— (1994), *Pedagogy of Hope*, New York: Continuum.

— (1997), 'A Response', in P. Freire, with J. W. Fraser, D. Macedo, T. McKinnon and W. T. Stokes (eds), *Mentoring the Mentor: A Critical Dialogue with Paulo Freire* (pp. 303–29), New York: Peter Lang.

— (1998a), *Teachers as Cultural Workers. Letters to Those Who Dare Teach*, Boulder, CO: Westview Press.

— (1998b), *Pedagogy of Freedom. Ethics, Democracy and Civic Courage*, Lanham, MD: Rowman & Littlefield.

— (1998c), *Politics and Education*, Los Angeles, CA: UCLA Latin American Center Publications.

Freire, P. and Macedo, D. (1987), *Literacy. Reading the Word and the World*, South Hadley, MA: Bergin and Garvey.
— (1993), 'A Dialogue with Paulo Freire', in P. McLaren and P. Leonard (eds), *Paulo Freire: A Critical Encounter* (pp. 169–76), New York and London: Routledge.
— (1995). 'A Dialogue: Culture, Language and Race', *Harvard Educational Review*, Vol. 65, No. 3, pp. 377–402.
Freire, P. and Faundez, A. (1989), *Learning to Question. A Pedagogy of Liberation*, Geneva: World Council of Churches.
Gadotti, M. (1994), *Reading Paulo Freire. His Life and Work*, Albany, NY: SUNY Press.
— (2005), 'Pedagogia da Terra e la cultura de sostenibilidad', *Revista Lusofona de Educacao*, Nu. 6.
— (2008), 'Educazione degli Adulti e Sviluppo delle Competenze: Una Visione basata sul Pensiero Critico', in F. Batini and A. Surian (eds), *Competenze e diritto all'Apprendimento*, Massa: Transeuropa.
Gadotti, M., Freire, P. and Guimarães, S. (1995), *Pedagogia: dialogo e conflitto* (B. Bellanova and F. Telleri, trans.), Torino: Societa Editrice Internazionale.
Gandin, L. A. and Apple, M. W. (2002), 'Thin versus Thick Democracy in Education: Porto Alegre and the Creation of Alternatives to Neo-Liberalism', *International Studies in Sociology of Education*, Vol. 12, No. 2, pp. 99–115.
Gelpi, E. (2002), *Lavoro Futuro. La formazione professionale come progetto politico*, Milan: Edizioni Angelo Guerini e Associati.
Gentili, P. (2005), *La Falsificazione del Consenso. Simulacro e Imposizione nella Riforma Educativa del Neoliberismo*, Pisa: Edizioni ETS.
Giroux, H. (1980a), 'Essay Review of Antonio Gramsci: Conservative Schooling for Radical Politics by Harold Entwistle', *Telos*, Vol. 45, pp. 215–25.
— (1980b), 'Gramsci, Hegemony, and Schooling', Review Symposium, *British Journal of Sociology of Education*, Vol. 13, No. 3, pp. 215–25.
— (1981a), *Ideology, Culture and the Process of Schooling*, Philadelphia, PA: Temple University Press.
— (1981b), 'Hegemony, Resistance and the Paradox of Educational Reform', *Interchange*, Vol. 12, Nos 2–3, pp. 3–26.
— (1983), *Theory and Resistance in Education: A Pedagogy for the Opposition*, Westport, CT: Bergin & Garvey.
— (1985), 'Introduction', in P. Freire, *The Politics of Education*, South Hadley, MA: Bergin & Garvey.

— (1988), *Teachers as Intellectuals: Towards a Critical Pedagogy of Learning*, Westport, CT: Bergin & Garvey.

— (1991), *Postmodernism, Feminism and Cultural Politics: Rethinking Educational Boundaries*, Albany, NY: SUNY Press.

— (1992), *Border Crossings: Cultural Workers and the Politics of Education*, New York: Routledge.

— (1993), *Living Dangerously: Multiculturalism and the Politics of Culture*, New York: Peter Lang.

— (1994a), *Disturbing Pleasures: Learning Popular Culture*, New York: Routledge.

— (1994b), 'Doing Cultural Studies: Youth and the Challenge of Pedagogy', *Harvard Educational Review*, Vol. 64, No. 3, pp. 247–77.

— (1996), *Fugitive Cultures*, New York: Routledge.

— (1997a), *Pedagogy and the Politics of Hope: Theory, Culture and Schooling*, Boulder, CO: Westview Press.

— (1997b), *Channel Surfing: Race Talk and the Destruction of Today's Youth*, New York: St. Martin's Press.

— (1999), *The Mouse That Roared: Disney and the End of Innocence*, Lanham, MD: Rowman & Littlefield.

— (2000a), *Impure Acts: The Practical Politics of Cultural Studies*, New York: Routledge.

— (2000b), *Stealing Innocence: Corporate Culture's War on Children*, New York: Palgrave.

— (2000c), 'Racial Politics, Pedagogy and the Crisis of Representation in Academic Multiculturalism', *Social Identities*, Vol. 6, No. 4, pp. 493–510.

— (2001), *Public Spaces/Private Lives: Beyond the Culture of Cynicism*, Lanham, MD: Rowman & Littlefield.

— (2002), *Breaking into the Movies, Film and the Culture of Politics*, Malden, MA: Blackwell.

— (2004), *The Terror of Neoliberalism. Authoritarianism and the Eclipse of Democracy*, Boulder, CO: Paradigm; Aurora, ON: Garamond Press.

— (2005a), *Against the New Authoritarianism. Politics after Abu Ghraib*, Winnipeg: Arbeiter Ring Publishing.

— (2005b), 'Cultural Studies in Dark Times: Public Pedagogy and the Challenge of Neoliberalism', *Fast Capitalism*, Vol. 1, No. 2, www.fastcapitalism.com/, accessed 2 February 2007.

— (2006a), *The Giroux Reader*, C. G. Robbins (ed.), Boulder, CO: Paradigm.

— (2006b), 'Culture, Politics and Pedagogy', Interview by J. Q. Adams, DVD, Northampton, MA: Media Education Foundation.

— (2006c), *Stormy Weather: Katrina and the Politics of Disposability*, Boulder, CO: Paradigm.

— (2006d), 'Katrina and the Politics of Disposability. News Reporting on the Aftermath of Katrina Blames the Victims Rather than Helps Them', *In These Times*, 14 September 2006, www.inthesetimes.com/site/main/article/2822/, accessed on 2 February 2007.

— (2006e), *Beyond the Spectacle of Terrorism. Global Uncertainty and the Challenge of the New Media*, Boulder, CO: Paradigm.

— (2006f), *America on the Edge. Henry Giroux on Politics, Culture, and Education*, Basingstoke and New York: Palgrave-Macmillan.

— (2007), *The University in Chains, Confronting the Military-Industrial-Academic Complex*, Boulder, CO: Paradigm.

— (2008), *Against the Terror of Neoliberalism: Politics Beyond the Age of Greed*, Boulder, CO: Paradigm.

— (2009a), 'The Politics of Lying and the Culture of Deceit in Obama's America. The Rule of Damaged Politics', *Truthout* 21 September 2009, www.truthout.org/092109R, accessed on 11October 2009.

— (2009b), 'Brutalising Kids: Painful Lessons in the Pedagogy of School Violence', *Truthout* 8 October 2009, www.truthout.org/10080912, accessed on 10 October 2009.

— (2009c), *Youth in a Suspect Society. Democracy or Disposability?* New York and London: Palgrave-Macmillan.

— (2009d), 'Town Hall Democracy or Mass Hysteria? Rethinking the Importance of the Public Sphere', *Truthout* 26 August 2009, www.truthout.org/082609L, accessed 12 October 2009.

— (2009e), 'The Spectacle of Illiteracy and the Crisis of Democracy', *Truthout* 15 September 2009, www.truthout.org/091509A, accessed 13 October 2009.

— (2010a), *Politics After Hope: Obama and the Crisis of Youth, Race, and Democracy*, Boulder, CO: Paradigm.

— (2010b), *Hearts of Darkness: Torturing Children in the War on Terrorism*, Boulder, CO: Paradigm.

Giroux, H. and McLaren, P. (eds) (1989), *Critical Pedagogy, the State and the Struggle for Culture*, Albany, NY: SUNY Press.

Giroux, H. and Simon, R. I. (eds) (1989), *Popular Culture, Schooling & Everyday Life*, Westport, CT: Bergin & Garvey.

Giroux, H. and Shannon, P. (eds) (1997), *Cultural Studies and Education Towards a Performative Practice*, New York: Routledge.

Giroux, H. and Giroux, S. S. (2004), *Take Back Higher Education. Race, Youth and the Crisis of Democracy in the Post-Civil Rights Era*, New York and Basingstoke: Palgrave-Macmillan.

Goulet, D. (1973), 'Introduction', in Freire, P., *Education for Critical Consciousness* (pp. vii–xiv), New York: Continuum.

Gramsci, A. (1971) *Selections for the Prison Notebooks* (Q. Hoare and G. Nowell Smith, trans. and eds), New York: International Publishers.

— (1972), *L'Alternativa Pedagogica*, M. A. Manacorda (ed.), Florence: La Nuova Italia.

— (1985). *Selections from* Cultural Writings, D. Forgacs and G. Nowell Smith (eds), H. Boelhower, trans., Cambridge, MA: Harvard University Press.

Gutierrez, F. and Prado, C. (2000), *Ecopedagogia e Cittadinanza Planetaria* (Ecopedagogy and Planetary Citizenship), Bologna: E.M.I.

Hall, B. L. (1973a), *Wakati wa Furaha: An Evaluation of a Radio Study Group Campaign*, Dar es Salaam: Dar es Institute for Adult Education.

— (1973b), *Voices for Development. Tanzania's Mass Education Campaigns*, Uppsala: Scandinavian Institute for African Studies.

— (1975), *Adult Education and the Development of Socialism in Tanzania*, Nairobi: East African Publishing House.

— (1998), '"Please Don't Bother the Canaries": Paulo Freire and the International Council for Adult Education', *Convergence (Tribute to Paulo Freire)*, Vol. 31, pp. 95–104.

Hall, B. L. and Clover, D. (2005), 'Social Movement Learning', in L. English (ed.), *International Encyclopedia of Adult Education*, New York and London: Palgrave Macmillan.

— (2006), 'Social Movement Learning', in R. Veira de Castro, A. V. Sancho and P. Guimarães (eds), *Adult Education. New Routes in a New Landscape*, Braga: University of Minho.

Hall, B. L and Kassam, Y. (1972), *Studies in Adult Education*, Dar es Salaam: Institute for Adult Education.

Hall, B. L., Mhaiki, Malya and Maganga (1972), *The 1971 Literacy Campaign Study*, Dar es Salaam: Institute of Adult Education.

Harasim, L. M. (1983), *Literacy and National Reconstruction in Guinea Bissau. A Critique of the Freirean Literacy Campaign*, PhD dissertation, University of Toronto.

Hardt, M. and Negri, A. (2000), *Empire*, Cambridge, MA: Harvard University Press.

— (2003), 'Foreword', in W. Fisher and T. Ponniah (eds), *Another World Is Possible. Popular Alternatives to Globalization at the World Social Forum*, London: Zed Books; Nova Scotia: Fernwood Publishers; Kuala Lumpur: SIRD; Cape Town: David Philip.

Harris, S. (2007), *The Governance of Education: How Neoliberalism Is Transforming Policy and Practice*, London: Continuum Publishing Group.

Holst, J. D. (2001), *Social Movements, Civil Society, and Radical Adult Education*, Westport, CT and London: Bergin & Garvey.

— (2002), *Social Movements, Civil Society, and Radical Adult Education*, Westport, CT and London: Bergin & Garvey.

Hooks, B. (1989), *Talking Back: Thinking Feminist, Thinking Black* (1st edn), Toronto, Ontario, Canada: Between the Lines..

— (1994), *Teaching to Transgress*, New York and London: Routledge.

Horton, M. and Freire, P. (1990), *We Make the Road by Walking. Conversations on Education and Social Change*, Philadelphia, PA: Temple University Press.

Ives, P. (2004), *Language and Hegemony in Gramsci*, London: Pluto Press; Winnipeg: Fernwood Publishing.

Kahn, R. (2006), 'Paulo Freire and Eco-Justice: Updating Pedagogy of the Oppressed for the Age of Ecological Calamity', *Freire Online Journal*, Vol. 1, No. 1, pp. 1–11, http://web.gseis.ucla.edu/~pfi/Journal_PFI/Articles_Freire/FreireEcoJustice_Kahn.pdf

Kane, L. (2001), *Popular Education and Social Change in Latin America*, London: Latin American Bureau.

Kapoor, D. (2009), 'Globalization, Dispossession and Subaltern Social Movements (SSM). Learning in the South', in A. Abdi and D. Kapoor (eds), *Global Perspectives on Adult Education* (pp. 71–92), London and New York: Palgrave Macmillan.

Kassam, Y. (1994), 'Julius Kambarage Nyerere (1922–)', *Prospects*, Vol. 24, pp. 247–59.

Kellner, D. (2001). 'Reading Giroux: Cultural studies, critical pedagogy, and radical democracy', in H. Giroux (ed.), *Public Spaces/Private Lives. Beyond the Culture of Cynicism*, Lanham, MD: Rowman & Littlefield.

Kellner, D. and Share, J. (2009), 'Critical Media Literacy and Radical Democracy', in M. W. Apple, W. Au and L. A. Gandin (eds), *The Routledge International Handbook of Critical Education*, New York and London: Routledge.

Kerka, S. (2005), 'Research Methods', in L. M. English (ed.), *International Encyclopedia of Adult Education*, London and New York: Palgrave-Macmillan.

Kirkwood, G. and Kirkwood, C. (1989), *Living Adult Education. Freire in Scotland*, Milton Keynes and Philadelphia, PA: Open University Press.

— (2011). *Living Adult Education. Freire in Scotland* (Rev. edn), Rotterdam & Taipei: Sense Publishers.

Landri, P. (2009), 'La Governance del Lifelong Learning in Europa', *Lifelong Lifewide Learning*, No. 13, pp. 37–44.

Latapí, P. (1988), 'Participatory Research. A New Research Paradigm?' *Alberta Journal of Educational Research*, Vol. XXXIV, pp. 310–19.

Ledwith, M. (1987), *Participation in Transformation*, Birmingham: Venture Press.

— (2005), *Community Development: A Critical Approach*, Bristol: Policy Press/BASW.

— (2010), 'Antonio Gramsci and Feminism: The Elusive Nature of Power', in P. Mayo (ed.), *Gramsci and Educational Thought*, Oxford: Wiley Blackwell.

Livingstone, D. W. (1976), 'On Hegemony in Corporate Capitalist States: Materialist Structures, Ideological forms, Class Consciousness and Hegemonic Acts', *Sociological Inquiry*, Vol. 46, No. 4, pp. 235–50.

— (1983), *Class, Ideologies & Educational Futures*, Sussex: The Falmer Press.

London and Edinburgh Weekend Return Group (1979, 1980), *In and Against the State*, Bristol: Pluto Press.

Löwy, M. and Betto, F. (2003), 'Values (1) Values of a New Civilisation', in W. Fisher and T. Ponniah (eds), *Another World Is Possible. Popular Alternatives to Globalization at the World Social Forum*, London: Zed Books; Nova Scotia: Fernwood Publishers; Kuala Lumpur: SIRD; Cape Town: David Philip.

Lucio-Villegas Ramos, E. (2004), 'Tejiendo la Ciudadania Desde la Educación', in E. Lucio-Villegas Ramos and P. Aparicio Guadas (eds), *Educación, democracia y partecipación*, Xativa, València: CREC.

Lucio-Villegas Ramos, E., García Florindo, A., García Goncet, D., Romeo Ortiz, E., Castaño Moreno, A., Fragoso, A. and Cowe, L. (2009), 'Educando la Ciudadania con el Telón de Fondo de los Presupuestos Participativos', in E. Lucio-Villegas Ramos (ed.), *La Ciudadanía como Creación politica y educativa. Educando para una ciudadanía Mundial*, Xàtiva, València: CREC.

Lyotard, J. (1989), *The Postmodern Condition. A Report on Knowledge*, Minneapolis, MN: University of Minnesota Press.

Macedo, D. (1994), *Literacies of Power*, Boulder, CO: Westview, Press.

Macedo, D. and Gounari, P. (eds) (2006), *The Globalization of Racism*, Boulder, CO: Paradigm.

Macedo, D., Dendrinos, B. and Gounari, P. (2003), *The Hegemony of English*, Boulder, CO: Paradigm.

McLaren, P. (1998), *Life in Schools. An Introduction to Critical Pedagogy in the Foundations of Education*, New York: Addison Wesley Longman.

— (2000), *Che, Freire and the Pedagogy of Revolution*, Lanham, MD: Rowman & Littlefield.

— (2002), Afterword, 'A Legacy of Hope and Struggle', in A. Darder, *Reinventing Paulo Freire. A Pedagogy of Love* (pp. 245–53), Boulder, CO: Westview Press.

McLaren, P. and Lankshear, C. (eds) (1994), *Politics of Liberation. Paths from Freire*, London and New York: Routledge.

McLaren, P. and Leonard, P. (eds) (1993), *Paulo Freire: A Critical Encounter*, London and New York: Routledge.

Malabotta, M. R. (2002), 'Education for a Multicultural Italy', *Journal of Postcolonial Education*, Vol. 1, No. 2, pp. 69–79.

Mannheim, K. (1936), *Ideology and Utopia* (L. Wirth and E. Shils, trans.), New York: Harcourt, Brace & World.

Marshall, J. (1997). 'Globalisation from Below. The Trade Union Connections', in S. Walters (ed.), *Globalization, Adult Education and Training. Impact and Issues* (pp. 57–68). London and New York: Zed Books; Leicester, UK: NIACE.

Martin, I. (1999), 'Introductory Essay: Popular Education and Social Movements in Scotland Today', in J. Crowther, I. Martin and M. Shaw (eds), *Popular Education and Social Movements in Scotland Today*, Leicester: NIACE.

— (2001), 'Reconstructing the Agora: Towards an Alternative Politics of Lifelong Learning', *Concept*, Vol. 11, No. 1, pp. 4–8.

Marx, K. and Engels, F. (1970), *The German Ideology*, C. J. Arthur (ed.), London: Lawrence and Wishart.

— (1848; 1998), *The Communist Manifesto. 150 Anniversary Edition*, New York and London: Monthly Review Press.

Mayo, M. (1997), *Imagining Tomorrow Adult Education for Transformation*, Leicester: NIACE.

Mayo, P. (1999), *Gramsci, Freire and Adult Education. Possibilities for Transformative Action*, London and New York: Zed Books.

— (2002), 'Public Pedagogy and the Quest for a Substantive Democracy' (Essay Review), *Interchange*, Vol. 33, No. 2, pp. 193–207.

— (2004), *Liberating Praxis. Paulo Freire's Legacy for Radical Education and Politics*, Westport, CT: Praeger.

— (2007), 'Critical Approaches to Education in the Work of Lorenzo Milani and Paulo Freire', *Studies in Philosophy and Education*, Vol. 26, No. 6, pp. 525–44.

— (2009), 'Competences and the Right to Learning', *LLinE (Lifelong Learning in Europe)*, Vol. XIV, No. 2, pp. 78–82.

— (2009), 'Competitiveness, Diversification and the International HE Cash Flow. EU's Higher Education Discourse Amidst the Challenges of Globalization', *International Studies in Sociology of Education*, Vol. 19, No. 2, pp. 85–100.

— (2010), *Liberating Praxis. Paulo Freire's legacy for Radical Education and Politics*, Rotterdam & Taipei: Sense Publishers.

Melo, A. (1985), 'From Traditional Cultures to Adult Education. The Portuguese experience After 1974', in K. Wain (ed.), *Lifelong Education and Participation* (pp. 38–48), Malta: University of Malta Press.

Milani, L. (1970), *Lettere di Don Lorenzo Milani*. Priore di Barbiana, Milan: Oscar Mondadori.

— (1988a), 'Letter of Don Lorenzo Milani to the Military Chaplains of Tuscany Who Signed the Communiqué of 11 February 1965', in J. T. Burtchaell (ed.), *A Just War no Longer Exists. The Teaching and Trial of Don Lorenzo Milani* (pp. 18–28), Notre Dame, IN: University of Notre Dame Press.

— (1988b), 'Milani's Letter to the Judges', in J. T. Burtchaell (ed.), *A Just War no Longer Exists. The Teaching and Trial of Don Lorenzo Milani* (pp. 52–77), Notre Dame, IN: University of Notre Dame Press.

— (1991), *L'Obbedienza Non è Più Una Virtu*, Florence: Libreria Editrice Fiorentina.

— (1996), *La Parola ai Poveri. Rilettura di Una Esperienza e di Una Testimonianza*, Fossano: Editrice Esperienze.

— (2004), *Una Lezione alla Scuola di Barbiana*, Florence: Libreria Editrice Fiorentina.

Morgagni, E. (1995), 'Anno 1989: Paulo Freire, "dottore in Pedagogia", honoris causa, dell' Alma Mater Studiorum di Bologna', in M. Gadotti, P. Freire and S. Guimarães, *Pedagogia: dialogo e conflitto* (B. Bellanova and F. Telleri, eds) (pp. 86–91), Torino: Società Editrice Internazionale.

Morrow, R. A. and Torres, C. A. (1995), *Social Theory and Education. A Critique of Theories of Social and Cultural Reproduction*, Albany, NY: SUNY Press.

— (2002), *Reading Freire and Habermas. Critical Pedagogy and Transformative Social Change*, New York and London: Teachers College Press.

Mushi, P. A. K. (1994), 'Literacy as Agricultural Development Strategy: The Tanzanian Experience', *Canadian Journal for the Study of Adult Education*, Vol. 8, pp. 65–72.

Newman, M. (1999, 2002, 2007), *Maeler's Regard. Images of Adult Learning*, Sydney, Australia: Centre for Popular Education UTS, www.michaelnewman.info.

Ngugi, W. T. (1986), *Decolonising the Mind: The Politics of Language in African Literature*, Nairobi, Kenya and London: Heinemann.

Nyerere, J. K. (1968), *Uhuru Na Ujamaa Freedom and Socialism*, London, Oxford and New York: Oxford University Press.

— (1974), *Man and Development Binadamu Na Maendeleo* (*sic*), London, Oxford and New York: Oxford University Press.

— (1977), *'The Arusha Declaration – Ten Years After'*, Dar es Salaam: Government Printer.

— (1979a), 'Relevance and Dar es Salaam University', in H. Hinzen and V. H. Hundsdorfer (Authors/Eds), *The Tanzanian Experience: Education for Liberation and Development*, Hamburg: UNESCO Institute for Education; London: Evans Brothers.

— (1979b), 'Adult Education and Development', in H. Hinzen and V. H. Hundsdorfer (Authors/Eds), *The Tanzanian Experience: Education for Liberation and Development*, Hamburg: UNESCO Institute for Education; London: Evans Brothers.

— (1979c), 'Our Education Must be for Liberation', in H. Hinzen and V. H. Hundsdorfer (Authors/Eds), *The Tanzanian Experience: Education for Liberation and Development*, Hamburg: UNESCO Institute for Education; London: Evans Brothers.

— (1979d), 'Education Never Ends', in H. Hinzen and V. H. Hundsdorfer (Authors/Eds), *The Tanzanian Experience: Education for Liberation and Development*, Hamburg: UNESCO Institute for Education; London: Evans Brothers.

— (1996), 'Working for Peace', Transcript of interview with Charlayne Hunter-Gault in A *News Hour* with Jim Lehrer (Online), 27 December, www.pbs.org/newshour/bb/africa/december96/nyerere_12–27.html

Obilade, O. (2005), 'Participatory Action Research', in L. English (ed.), *International Encyclopedia of Adult Education*, New York and London: Palgrave Macmillan.

O'Cadiz, P., Wong, P. L. and Torres, C. A. (1997), *Education and Democracy. Paulo Freire, Social Movements and Educational Reform in São Paulo*, Boulder, CO: Westview Press.

— (1998). *Education and Democracy. Paulo Freire, Social Movements and Educational Reform in São Paulo*, Boulder, CO: Westview Press.

OECD (1996), *Lifelong Learning for All*, Paris, France: Organisation for Economic Development and Cooperation.

— (2007), *Lifelong Learning and Human Capital (sic) Policy Brief*, Paris, France: Organisation for Economic Development and Cooperation.

Okoh, J. D. (1980), *Julius Nyerere's Social Philosophy and Its Implications for Education*, PhD dissertation, Department of Educational Foundations, University of Alberta.

OSAL (Latin American Social Observatory) and CLACSO (Latin American Social Science Council) (2003), 'The Global Civil Society Movement (1) Discussion Document', in W. Fisher and T. Ponniah, *Another World Is Possible. Popular Alternatives to Globalization at the World Social Forum*, London: Zed Books; Nova Scotia: Fernwood Publishers; Kuala Lumpur: SIRD; Cape Town: David Philip.

Park, P., Brydon-Miller, M., Hall, B. L. and Jackson, T. (eds) (1993), *Voices of Change: Participatory Research in the United States and Canada*, Toronto: OISE Press.

Pecorini, G. (1998), *Don Milani. Chi era Costui?* Milan: Baldini & Castoldi.

Ponniah, T. and Fisher, W. F. (2003), 'Introduction. The World Social Forum and the Reinvention of Democracy', in W. Fisher and T. Ponniah (2003), *Another World Is Possible. Popular Alternatives to Globalization at the World Social Forum*, London: Zed Books; Nova Scotia: Fernwood Publishers; Kuala Lumpur: SIRD; Cape Town: David Philip.

Riley, T. and Hawe, P. (2004), 'Researching Practice: The Methodological Case for Narrative Inquiry', *Health Education Research*, Vol. 20, No. 2, pp. 226–36.

Roberts, P. (ed.) (1999), *Paulo Freire, Politics and Pedagogy: Reflections from Aotearoa-New Zealand*, Palmerston North: Dunmore Press.

— (2000), *Education, Literacy, and Humanization Exploring the Work of Paulo Freire*, Westport, CT: Bergin & Garvey.

Rossatto, C. A. (2005), *Engaging Paulo Freire's Pedagogy of Possibility. From Blind to Transformative Optimism*, Lanham, MD: Rowman & Littlefield.

Said, E. (1978), *Orientalism*, New York: Random House.

— (1993), *Culture and Imperialism*, London: Vintage.

Samoff, J. (1990), '"Modernizing" a Socialist Vision: Education in Tanzania', in M. Carnoy and J. Samoff (eds), *Education and Social Transition in the Third World*, Princeton, NJ: Princeton University Press.

Schirru, G. (ed.) (2009), 'Gramsci, le Culture e il Mondo', Atti del convegno internazionale organizzato da Fondazione Istituto Gramsci, International

Gramsci Society-Italia, Roma 27–28 April 2007, Rome: Viella Libreria Editrice.

Schugurensky, D. (1998), 'The Legacy of Paulo Freire. A Critical Review of His Contributions', *Convergence*, Vol. XXI, Nos 1 and 2, pp. 17–29.

— (2002), 'Transformative Learning and Transformative Politics. The Pedagogical Dimension of Participatory Democracy and Social Action', in E. O'Sullivan, A. Morrell and M. A. O'Connor (eds), *Expanding the Boundaries of Transformative Learning. Essays on Theory and Praxis*, New York and Basingstoke: Palgrave.

— (2011), *Paulo Freire*, New York and London: Continuum.

Scuola di Barbiana (1996), *Lettera A Una Professoressa*, Florence: Libreria Editrice Fiorentina.

Shiva, V. (2003), 'The Living Democracy Movement: Alternatives to the Bankruptcy of Globalization', in W. Fisher and T. Ponniah (2003), *Another World Is Possible. Popular Alternatives to Globalization at the World Social Forum*, London: Zed Books; Nova Scotia: Fernwood Publishers; Kuala Lumpur: SIRD; Cape Town: David Philip.

Shor, I. (1980, 1987), *Critical Teaching in Everyday Life*, Chicago, IL: University of Chicago Press.

— (ed.) (1987), *Freire for the Classroom*, Portsmouth, NH: Boynton/Cook.

— (1992), *Empowering Education. Critical Teaching for Social Change*, Chicago, IL: University of Chicago Press.

Shor, I. and Freire, P. (1987), *Pedagogy for Liberation Dialogues on Transforming Education*, South Hadley, MA: Bergin and Garvey.

Simeone, D. (1996), *Verso la Scuola di Barbiana. L'esperienza pastorale educativa di don Lorenzo Milani a S. Donato di Calenzano*, San Pietro in Cariano (Verona): Il Segno dei Gabrielli Editori.

Smith, M. K. (1999), *Julius Nyerere, Lifelong Learning and Informal Education*, www.infed.org/thinkers/et-nye.htm

Stédile, J. P. and Fernandes, B. M. (2001), *Brava Gente. La Lunga Marcia del Movimento Senza Terra del Brasile dal 1984 al 2000*, Rome: Rete Radié Resch

Streck, D., Redin, E. and Zitkoski, J. J. (eds) (2010), *Dicionário Paulo Freire*, Belo Horizonte: Autêntica Editora.

Sultana, R. G. (2009), 'Competences and Competence Frameworks in Career Guidance: Complex and Contested Concepts', *International Journal of Educational Vocational Guidance*, Vol. 9, pp. 15–30.

Sumra, S. and Bwatwa, Y. D. M. (1988), 'Adult Education, Literacy Training and Skill Upgrading in Tanzania', *The Alberta Journal of Educational Research*, Vol. 34, pp. 259–68.

Surian, A. (2006), 'Gli orientamenti degli Organismi internazionali sulla valutazione dell'istruzione superiore', in R. Semeraro (ed.), *Valutazione e qualità della didattica universitaria. Le prospettive nazionali e internazionali*, Milan: Franco Angeli.

Tandon, R. (2000a), 'Civil Society, Adult Learning and Action in India', *Convergence*, Vol. 33, Nos 1 and 2, pp. 120–37.

— (2000b), 'Riding High or Nosediving: Development NGOs in the New Millennium', *Development in Practice*, Vol. 10, Nos 3 and 4, pp. 319–29.

— (2003), *Does Civil Society Matter? Governance in Contemporary India*, New Delhi and New York: Sage.

Taylor, P. V. (1993), *The Texts of Paulo Freire*, Buckinghamshire: Open University Press.

Thompson, J. L. (ed.) (1980), *Adult Education for a Change*, Hutchinson, KS: Kent.

— (2000), *Stretching the Academy. The Politics and Practice of Widening Participation in Higher Education*, Leicester: NIACE.

Torres, C. A. (1982), 'From the Pedagogy of the Oppressed to a Luta Continua – The Political Pedagogy of Paulo Freire', *Education with Production*, Vol. 2, pp. 76–97.

— (1998), *Education, Power, and Personal Biography: Dialogues with Critical Educators*, New York: Routledge.

— (2009), *Globalizations and Education. Collected Essays on Class, Race, Gender, and the State*, New York: Teachers College Press.

Torres, C. A. and Nogueira, P. (eds) (2008), *Social Justice Education for Teachers. Freire and the Possible Dream*, Rotterdam/Taipei: Sense Publishers.

Unsicker, J. (1986), 'Tanzania's Literacy Campaign in Historical-Structural Perspective', in R. F. Arnove and H. Graff (eds), *National Literacy Campaigns in Historical and Comparative Perspective*, New York: Plenum.

Vella, J. (1996). 'Getting Them On While Keeping Them In. Education and the Politics of Incarceration', Unpublished Master's dissertation, University of Malta.

Von Freyhold (1979), 'Some Observations on Adult Education in Tanzania', in H. Hinzen and V. H. Hundsdorfer (Authors/Eds), *The Tanzanian Experience: Education for Liberation and Development*, Hamburg: UNESCO Institute for Education; London: Evans Brothers.

Wain, K. (2004a), 'Lifelong Learning: Some Critical Reflections', in D. Caruana and P. Mayo (eds), *Perspectives on Lifelong Learning in the Mediterranean*, Bonn: IIZ-DVV.

— (2004b), *The Learning Society in a Postmodern World. The Education Crisis*, New York and London: Peter Lang.

Webster, L. and Mertova, P. (2007), *Using Narrative Inquiry as a Research Method: An Introduction to Using Critical Event Narrative Analysis in Research on Learning and Teaching*, Oxford and New York: Routledge.

Welton, M. (1993), 'Social Revolutionary Learning: The New Social Movements as Learning Sites', *Adult Education Quarterly*, Vol. 43, No. 3, pp. 152–64.

Williams, R. (1993), 'Adult Education and Social Change', in J. McIlroy and S. Westwood (eds), *Border Country: Raymond Williams in Adult Education* (pp. 255–64), Leicester: NIACE.

Williamson, B. (1998), *Lifeworlds and Learning. Essays in the Theory, Philosophy and Practice of Lifelong Learning*, Leicester: NIACE.

Winterton, J., Delamare-Le Deist, F. and Stringfellow, E. (2005), *Typology of Knowledge, Skills and Competences: Clarification of the Concept and Prototype* (Panorama Series, No. 1397), Luxembourg: Office for Official Publications of the European Communities.

Youngman, F. (1986), *Adult Education and Socialist Pedagogy*, London: Routledge Kegan Paul.

— (2000), *Political Economy of Adult Education and Development*, London: Zed Books.

Author Index

Subject Index